TOO CLOSE FOR COMFORT

This book is to be returned on or before the last date stamped below.

Too Close for Comfort

Joy Hayward and David Carlyle

TOO CLOSE FOR COMFORT

A book about teenagers who have been sexually abused within their families

Joy Hayward
and
David Carlyle

LDA

Too Close for Comfort
LD609
ISBN 1 85503 074 8
© Longman Paul
First published 1988 by Longman Paul Limited, New Zealand
This edition first published 1991
Reprinted 1991
All rights reserved
Illustrations by Sally Hollis McLeod
Cover Illustration by Tony Randell

LDA, Duke Street, Wisbech, Cambs. PE13 2AE

Printed by Bell and Bain Ltd., Glasgow

Contents

Preface
Introduction 1

Part One 3
Pania 5
Sharon 19
Christopher 31
Natasha 51

Part Two 77
What is 'it'? 79
The most untalked about subject in the world 81
Why did he do it? 83
Why did she let him? 85

Feelings you might have: 87
   It is just not worth trusting people 87
   No one in the world believes me 88
   Alone in the world 90
   Worth nothing to no one 92
   Shame 93
   I feel like I have to keep this rage inside me for ever 96
   Men – yuk! 100
   I feel I have lost everything, even myself 104
   I feel responsible 106
   I don't know how I feel 108
   Hurting yourself – the cut so deep 110

Ways of getting by: 112
   1 Sweeping it under the carpet 112
   2 Being a shop window 114
   3 Being in sole charge 114
   4 Clinging on for dear life 115
   5 Telling, but not in words 116
   6 Killing the pain 116
   7 Filling the hole 116
   8 Starving to death 118
   9 Holding on tight 118
  10 Keeping the boat steady 119
  11 Being in the same boat 120
  12 Trapped into becoming a care-giver 120
  13 Sleeping around 122
  14 Being a goody two shoes 123
  15 Blending in with the wallpaper 123
  16 Standing out like a sore thumb 124
  17 Keeping the lid on the pressure cooker 124
  18 Creating a war zone 124

What you can do now – A road map you can use 126
   1 Stop lying to yourself 127
   2 Stop managing so "well" and controlling yourself 130
   3 Become "selfish" 130
   4 Recognise your own "self worth" 132
   5 Challenge your fears 132
   6 Get some help 133

Glossary of terms 136

Useful addresses 139

Dedication

This book is dedicated to the people who attended our individual and group therapy sessions. Together we shared the pain of opening the wounds, the hardship of the struggle to heal, the pleasure of achievements, the disappointment of set-backs and the delight in successes. You helped us to gain insight and understanding, appreciation of the creative ways you used to keep surviving and the courage and strength you needed to keep going. Being part of that struggle often felt difficult, but it was always a real privilege.

Acknowledgements

We would like to thank:
Rhondda McLean for her willingness and patience in deciphering our handwriting and her excellent typing, often at short notice; Kevin Hayward for his willingness to take on extra housework and child-care to facilitate the finishing of this book; Joan Baker, Sue Bathgate, Anna and Malcolm Byford, Clare Dorking, Brian Miller, Liz Muir, Lizzie and Graham Price who offered invaluable encouragement, ideas, and support; and those others who have offered suggestions, cups of tea, back rubs, and time to listen to us agonise.

Preface to the British Edition

Alterations to the text for the British edition of "Too Close For Comfort" have only been made where cultural differences rendered it inappropriate, where the language used might have hindered comprehension, or where British procedure differs from that in New Zealand.

The stories in this book bear a great deal of resemblance to a great number of people we have worked with. They are, however, made up, as are all the names.

Introduction

This is a book for and about teenagers who have been sexually abused by someone in their families.

This is an experience both girls and boys have. Abusers can be men or women but most often they are men. This is why the abusers in Part One of this book are men. However, most of the points made in Part Two are just as relevant to someone who has been abused by a woman as to someone who has been abused by a man.

Maybe this is something that has happened to you, to someone in your family, or to one of your friends. If you decide to read on, this book could change your life.

Warning

Part One of this book has been written as a twist-a-plot. It is not intended to be read straight through from beginning to end. These pages tell the stories of Pania, Sharon, Christopher and Natasha. As you read you will be confronted with the choices they have to make. Choose carefully since your choice may lead to success or disaster, safety or danger.

What happens is a result of your choice. None of the choices is easy. Making choices that lead to safety and happiness will often seem impossible. There are happy endings but often you have to give up a lot on the way.

After you make your choice follow the instructions to see what happens next. Remember – some choices are irreversible. Think carefully before you make your move.

On page 136 there is a glossary for you to use if you do not fully understand some of the words that appear in this book.

Part ONE

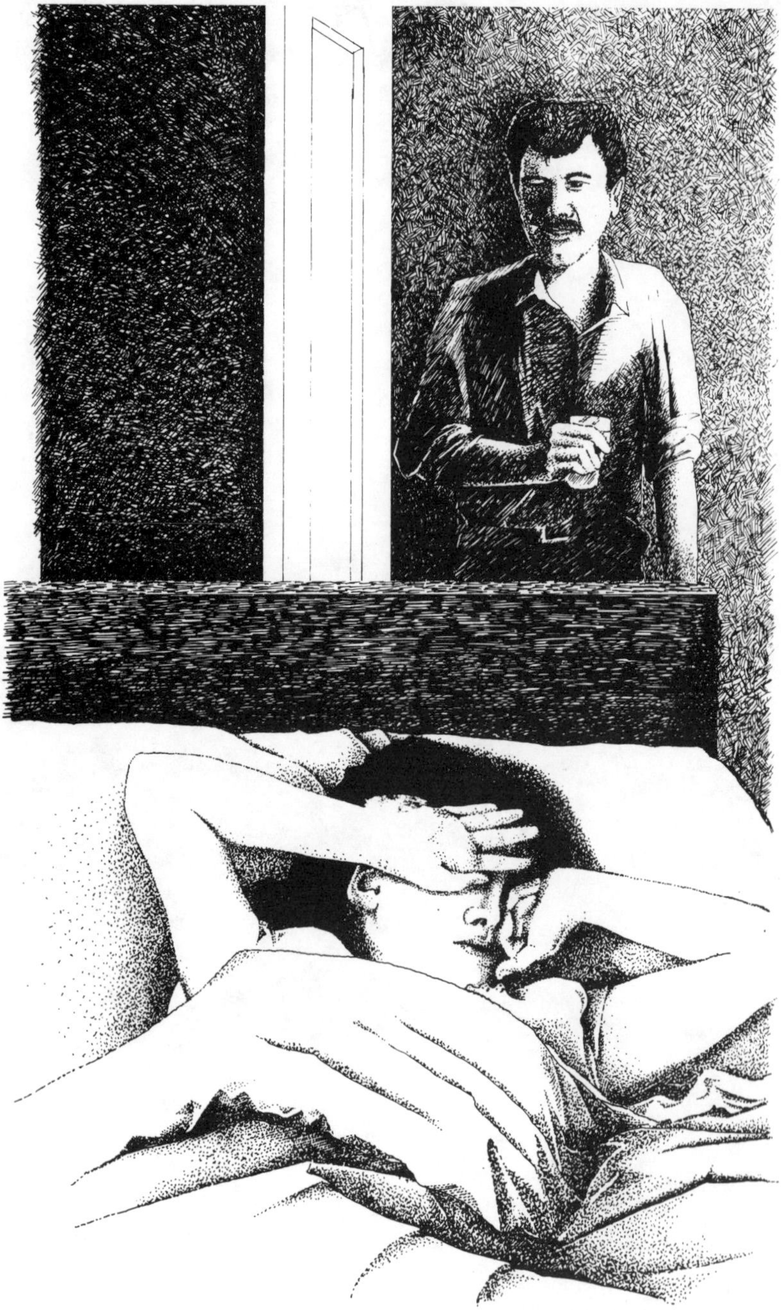

Pania

Pania went to live with her grandmother as a baby. Her own mother was working in the city.

Pania's grandmother had brought up lots of children and she was good at this. Grandmother was strict, sometimes Pania thought she was really fierce, and she was a little afraid of her. At other times though, she would be soft and quiet and Pania would snuggle up beside her.

When Pania was 5 her mother got married to Jim. It was exciting. There were lots of relatives and there was heaps to eat and drink. She and the other kids danced and played until they were exhausted. Pania could still hear people singing and laughing as she fell asleep in the corner.

In the next five years Mum and Jim had three children. Pania went to visit occasionally. It was fun to play with the little kids and have them clamour for her attention. But things were often strained between Mum and Jim and she was always pleased to go home.

It was a real shock when grandmother announced that she thought the family should all be together now. The thought of leaving grandmother seemed impossible.

The worst was yet to come. Mum said she had to be part of this family now. Grandmother was too old to be bothered with kids any more and she couldn't visit her.

Pania told herself it was good to be part of a family, but she had to stop her legs taking her back to her grandmother. Pania often felt really angry, but when she let people know about this she was sent to her room. This was really confusing as her mother and stepfather seemed to be always letting each other know they were angry.

One night when Pania was in bed they had a really big fight and Mum stormed out. She could hear Jim go to the cupboard and get the bottle of whisky out. Then everything went quiet.

She was just dozing off when she became aware that Jim was standing next to the bed. He lay down beside her and said he needed a cuddle. Then he put his hands under her nightie. She tried to pull away but he held on to her and told her this is what all fathers and daughters do, and since her own father wasn't around he would do it instead.

He lay on top of her and repeatedly forced her to have sexual intercourse. The pain was terrible. Afterwards she discovered she was bleeding and thought she was going to die. She felt really awful and desperately wanted her grandmother.

Going to school was a way of getting out of the house, but it was hard to concentrate on her work. She constantly left her homework behind, forgot how to spell, and had to sit out during Games lessons because she was too sore.

She tried to find out from friends if it was happening to them, but it was hard to discuss and they didn't seem to understand. She felt different and more and more alone.

When she was gathering her books up after school one day her form teacher, Mrs Costello, approached her. She had noticed how quiet and pre-occupied Pania seemed to be and wondered if anything was the matter. When Pania just shrugged, Mrs Costello said she had been concerned about her and thought there might be something wrong at home.

That night Pania was in turmoil. She was amazed Mrs Costello had noticed her. It had been really tempting to come straight out with it and tell her, but instead she had become frozen on the spot.

Telling seemed really scary, but the thought of her stepfather lying on top of her was suffocating. The thought that it would go on for ever was unbearable.

Telling would be a real relief but what would he do if

she did? What would her mother think? What if everyone at school found out? What would happen to her?

What would you do? If you think Pania should tell, turn to page 10.
If you think she should keep quiet, turn to page 8.

The next day after school Pania made sure she got out of the classroom the minute the bell went. She tried not to think of Mrs Costello, but found herself doing so after each time her stepfather visited her room.

She often had stomach cramps and her heart would race. She felt clumsy and was always dropping things. It was worst when she had her period. The blood reminded her of the first time and she still felt she might die and wondered if it might not be better if she did. She tried to explain to him at these times and hoped he would leave her alone, but usually it didn't work.

At times she noticed him making eyes at her little sister, Louise, who was now eight. She wondered if it was happening to her but told herself she was imagining it. Recently though, he was being really nice to Louise and the thought wouldn't go away.

The thought of telling started coming back into her mind, but how could she tell after all this time? Would people say she was stupid? Would anyone believe her now? If she didn't tell would he start doing it to Louise as well? Maybe he had already started.

What would you do?
If you think Pania should tell, turn to page 10.
If you think she shouldn't, turn to page 9.

It was impossible, Pania knew it. If she had told when she was 11 or even 12, or 13, maybe people wouldn't have blamed her because she was too young to know better. 15-year-olds were almost adult though and were meant to be able to deal with things so much better.

If Jim was having sex with her sister then Pania felt that would be her fault too. She was older, she should have been able to stop that happening. She felt she was such a hopeless, incompetent person. Feeling so bad inside, she thought she deserved to have this happening to her.

At school she became more alone. She was so wrapped up in her misery it became impossible to speak to her classmates. Feeling so worthless and awful she believed they wouldn't want to speak to her anyway; it was easier to be alone. Lunchtimes were the most difficult; sometimes she ate her lunch in the toilet. Once people were moving about after lunch it was easy to lose herself in the crowd.

She wanted to die. She thought it would be better for everyone if she were dead. Sometimes she thought she might die – her shoulders had weights on them, her stomach was in knots, she often found it hard to breathe, and when she had her period she bled and bled and throbbed all over.

At night she prayed she wouldn't wake up in the morning but she always did. She supposed God planned to make her die slowly since she was so bad.

She wondered how she could kill herself to speed up what seemed inevitable. It seemed the only way to stop the pain. But what if it didn't work? Her mind worked overtime thinking of what would happen if it didn't quite come off.

Just before Christmas she saw Mrs Costello in town. When she got home she thought again of telling. In her bag she had packets of pills from the cupboard at home. For hours she wavered between telling and taking the pills.

If you think Pania should tell, turn to page 10.
If you think she should take the pills, turn to page 16.

The next day when the last class finished Pania slowly packed her books. The other teenagers noisily hurried out into the afternoon. She kept wondering if she was doing the right thing. The knots in her stomach tightened as she glanced toward the front of the room. Mrs Costello was still there and their eyes met. Pania quickly went back to her books. She felt a sudden urge to run away, but her feet seemed nailed to the floor.

Then she heard Mrs Costello approaching. Her body felt as if it was turning to ice, but she knew that she was going to go through with this.

Mrs Costello's voice seemed reassuring. 'Would you like to stay and talk, Pania?' she said.

Pania could only nod.

'I have noticed you looking really miserable lately,' continued Mrs Costello.

Pania wanted to tell Mrs Costello how miserable she really was but no words would come. She suddenly found she had tears pouring down her face.

Mrs Costello sat down beside Pania, close but not touching. It was a long time before Pania could say anything but Mrs Costello waited and didn't go away.

It felt as if it had been years since she had cried, but now that the dam had broken Pania felt a mixture of fear and relief. Slowly she found words to go with the tears.

'I–I can't sleep at night, and I–have horrible nightmares.'

'Yes, nightmares can be really scary,' replied Mrs Costello.

'They are awful. I dream I am being suffocated,' continued Pania.

'Sometimes when people have scary nightmares it is because there is something happening when they are awake that frightens them,' said Mrs Costello.

Pania knew what she meant.

'It is my stepfather, I hate him.

Pania heard the words but it was as if they came from someone else, as if they didn't belong to her. The cold icy

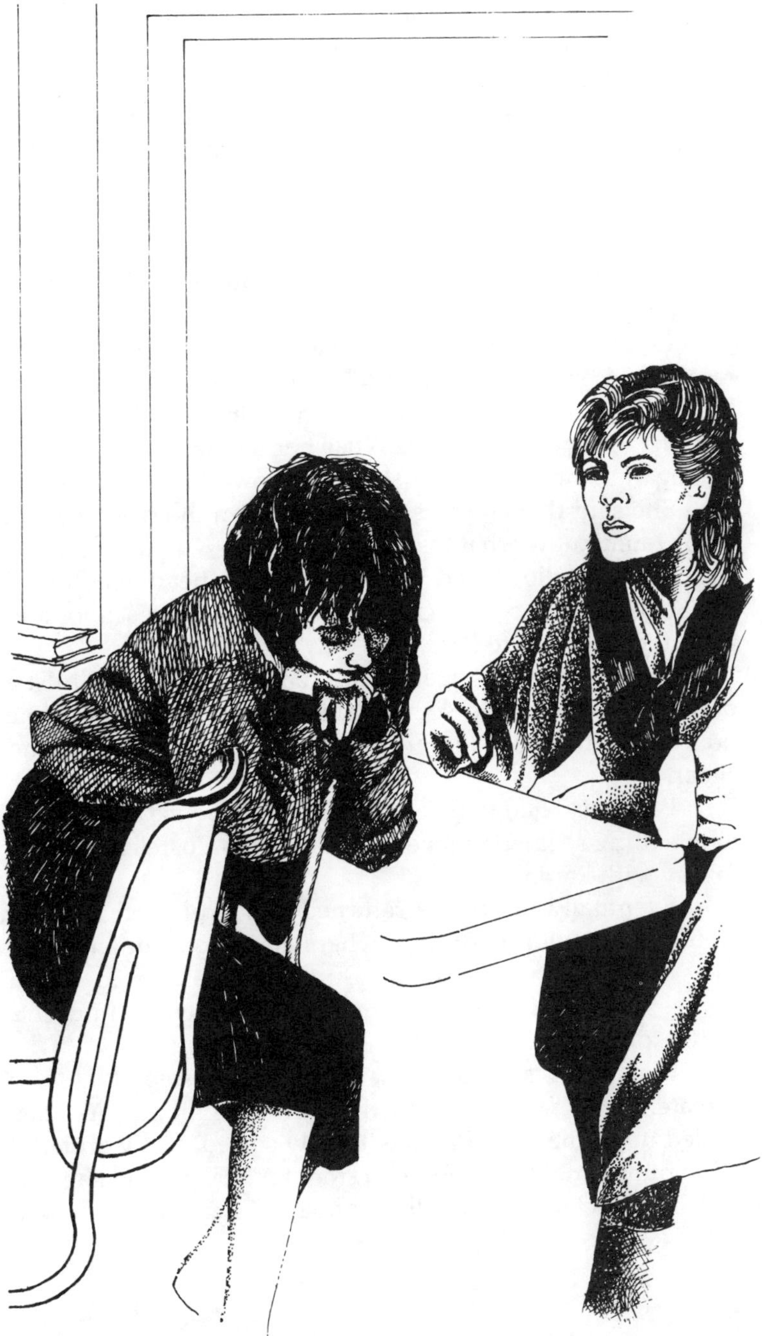

feeling returned to her body, but it all seemed so far away. Pania had been staring blankly at the floor for several minutes when Mrs Costello broke the silence.

'It seems like saying you hated your stepfather has taken all your energy away. Has he hurt you in some way?'

Mrs Costello's voice came like a safety line thrown into the void. Pania clung to it as the words 'Has he hurt you?' echoed around her.

'Yes, he – he comes to my room at night and he touches me.'

Once the words were out, Pania felt ashamed, embarrassed and expected Mrs Costello to look shocked, or to tell her she was being silly. Instead she calmly told Pania she couldn't keep this a secret. What her stepfather was doing was against the law and must not be allowed to continue.

She said that she was going to inform the headteacher, who would know what to do.

Mrs Costello stayed with Pania as the head telephoned the Social Services. A social worker came to the school and introduced herself to Pania.

Then they went together to the Police Station. Whilst a policewoman and the social worker talked to Pania, some police officers went to interview her stepfather, mother, and sister.

Pania also had to be examined by the police doctor. The whole thing seemed to take hours, but Mrs Costello was able to stay with Pania.

Eventually the police returned and explained that her stepfather wouldn't admit to what had happened, and until they could go to court Pania would not be able to return home. She would have to go into a Social Services children's centre to keep her safe.

When her sisters were naughty her stepfather had threatened to send them to the children's home. As they pulled up at the door Pania felt really scared. She wondered what punishments would be in store for her. Instead she was met by a social worker called Linda Pullinger who showed her around, introduced her to the other staff and girls, and organised a meal for her.

During her time at the girls' centre Pania felt very up and down. Sometimes she felt that she had nothing to live for. She would lie awake for hours each night before she could sleep, but when she woke in the morning she wished she could stay asleep for ever.

When she did sleep that was usually awful too. Jim often appeared in her dreams but he would quickly vanish again.

At other times she felt brighter. It was a relief to feel safe from her stepfather. The staff seemed to know what she was going through. She also saw a counsellor once a week who understood and helped her to deal with the difficult feelings.

The court date seemed a long way off. She dreaded having to stand up in court and explain to everyone what had happened. If her stepfather wasn't convicted she wouldn't ever be able to go back home. She wasn't really sure she ever wanted to.

Pania hoped her mother would support her, but knew in her heart she wouldn't. Phone calls with her had been really difficult. She had accused Pania of lying and bringing shame on the family. She had told her she would never be forgiven if she went to court.

Pania felt torn in two. The social worker, Mrs Costello and the counsellor all encouraged her to go to court, but how could she? From the time she could talk she had learnt that obedience to parents came before everything else. She had to try to blot out 15 years of these messages. They were so strong, they had never been questioned.

The court day came. Pania hadn't been able to sleep at all the previous night. She lay in bed wishing she had never told and right up until the last minute didn't know whether she could go through with it.

Afterwards she wasn't sure how she had managed. At first it seemed unreal.

Pania's evidence was heard first. It had all been written down by the police. This record (called a statement) had been taken to the first hearing, but this time Pania had to appear and give evidence herself.

First her lawyer (the prosecution lawyer) asked her questions, and then the lawyer who was acting for her stepfather (the defence lawyer) asked her more questions. Pania answered each question, but although she knew the words were coming out of her mouth, she felt they weren't connected to her.

Once Pania left the stand, other witnesses were called and cross-examined.

The prosecution and the defence presented their cases. Witnesses were called and cross-examined. The doctor gave her evidence, which took quite a long time. The Social Welfare Department, Mrs Costello, and the counsellor all gave their evidence.

It wasn't until Jim took the stand that Pania started to believe it wasn't just part of the dream. She couldn't bring herself to look at him when he spoke, but as she heard the lies he told she wanted to explode.

Worse still was listening to her mother. Her words washed over her but she felt betrayed, and as if she had been kicked in the guts.

When it was her turn to speak the words came out, but Pania again had the sensation that they weren't connected to her.

At the end of it all the judge ruled that, in his opinion, she had been sexually assaulted by her stepfather. Jim was convicted and sentenced to two years in prison.

The court case was all over but it seemed things were just beginning. Everyone had to make a new life for themselves.

Pania was going to live with foster-parents. It was much smaller than the girls' centre and she could stay there until she was old enough to live on her own. Becoming part of a new family was difficult at first. She was really scared of upsetting her foster-parents and worried that she would do or say the wrong thing. They seemed, however, to continue to like her even when she didn't get things quite right.

Pania still visited her family sometimes. It was different now her stepfather wasn't there, but the atmosphere was still uncomfortable and she was usually pleased to get back to her new home.

She still felt very lonely sometimes, but it seemed she wasn't alone quite so often these days. Since she had started talking, at first with Mrs Costello, then with the people at the girls' centre and with her counsellor, it had become easier to talk to her classmates.

Making friends hadn't happened overnight. Pania was too scared to put much trust in people and she felt there was a lot of her she needed to keep to herself, but it was nice to be included, to be invited to the pictures, skating, dancing, and town on Friday nights.

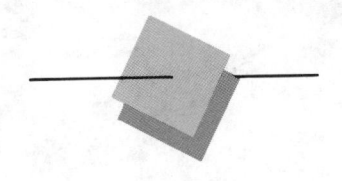

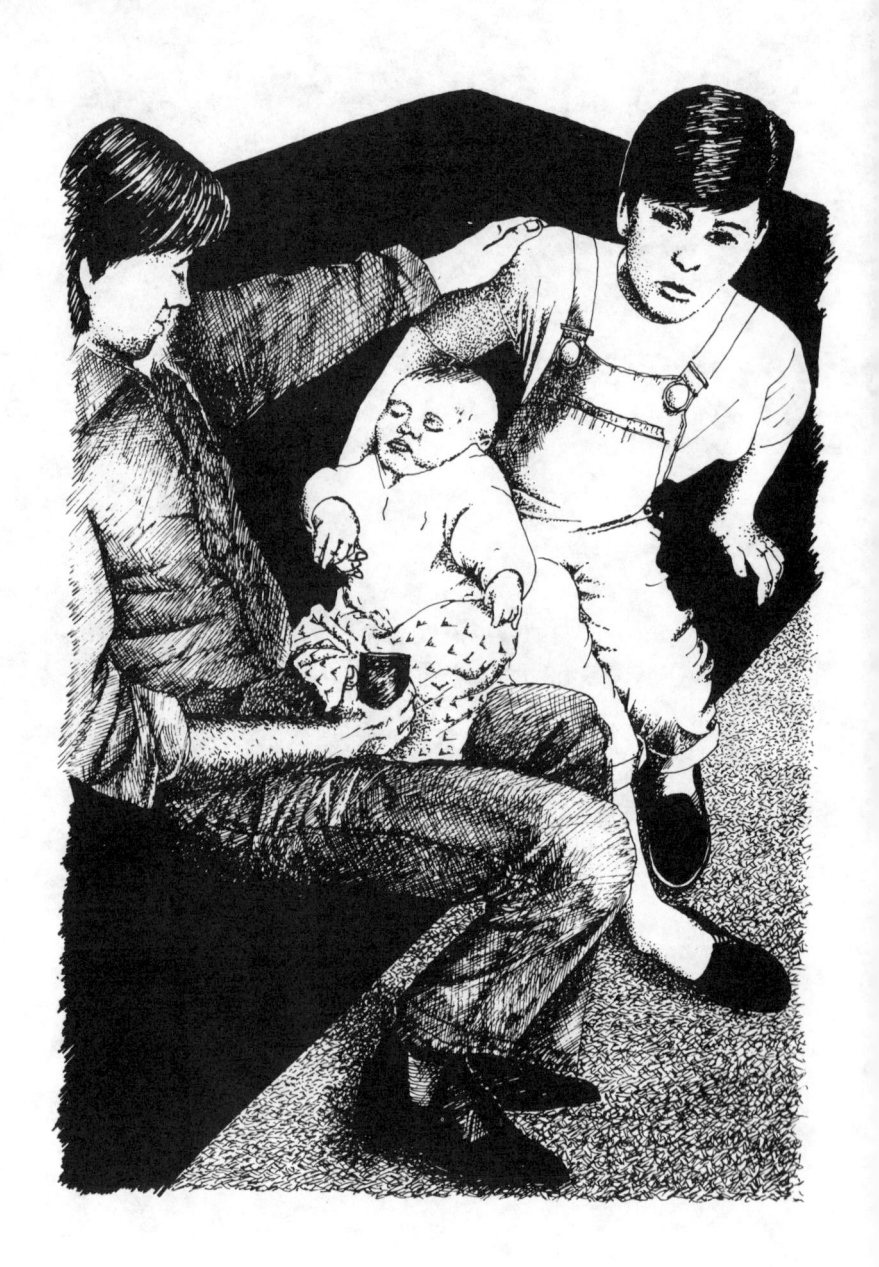

Sharon

Sharon couldn't remember her mother ever being well. From the time she was little it seemed she was always being told 'Keep quiet, your mother has a headache' or 'Be especially good today, your mother has had a bad night.'

Sometimes she used to sit on Mum's bed and they would read stories and sing songs. If she got too noisy or boisterous her mother would say she needed to rest again now and would Sharon please go outside and play for a while.

Sharon remembered her fifth birthday. She was a big girl now – old enough to be a school girl. Being grown up (well almost) meant she would be much more able to look after Mum. She learnt how to make cups of tea, fill her hot water bottles, and brush her hair. Maybe if she looked after her really well Mum would get strong and healthy.

There had been times when Mum had been well enough to be up and about. Sharon remembered a time when they had gone to the beach – her and Mum and Dad – all three of them together. They had built huge sand castles, played in the water, climbed on the rocks and bought strawberry ice-creams. She had wished that day would last for ever.

When Sharon was 11 Mum unexpectedly became pregnant. Sharon was delighted at the thought of having a baby in the house. Mum didn't share her delight and was really ill for most of the pregnancy.

The birth was difficult and the next day Mum looked

really awful, but the baby was beautiful and Sharon helped to choose his name. They decided to call him Lee.

There were times though, when Mum seemed to enjoy the baby, but she found him really tiring and was pleased to be able to hand over to Sharon when she came home from school. Sharon became an expert at bathing and feeding him, changing his nappies, and devising all kinds of entertainments for him. She also took over a lot of the household chores to relieve Mum of the burden.

At secondary school this became more difficult. There was so much else to do, like homework and going out with friends. Unlike going out at primary school, teenage outings were a lot more sophisticated. First, there was the matter of deciding what clothes to wear, what kind of hairstyle, whether to wear studs or dangly ear-rings, and how much make-up it was possible to get away with without parents insisting it be washed off.

Sharon spent hours in front of the mirror dressing and undressing, examining herself from every angle, with and without clothes on. It had been a struggle to get used to an adult body. At first it had been embarrassing. Sharon had started to develop long before the others in her class. Kids used to ping her bra and try to match her up with male student teachers. Thinking she was the only one having a period was just awful. She was sure everyone would know. Tampons were hard to get used to, and pads just had to be noticed at PE or Games. It had been a real surprise and relief when she discovered most of her friends felt exactly the same.

Nowadays though, she could enjoy her breasts, although periods were still a bit of a hassle, and it was fun to explore her 'new' body and to feel excited as she touched her genitals. Now she chose clothes to show off, rather than camouflage, her new body.

Often though, when she emerged from her room, she would realise that she had been needed to help, and wished she hadn't been so involved with herself. Going out was difficult too, especially if she was invited to stay overnight or go away for the weekend. Everyone told her to go and enjoy herself but she always felt a bit guilty about leaving Mum to manage on her own.

When Lee was two, however, Sharon again became involved in full-time helping. Mum had to go back into hospital. Lee went to a child-care centre. Sharon collected him each day after school and they both went to visit Mum. Sharon tried to keep her spirits up by taking her flowers, telling her jokes, and the latest stories about old Buggerlugs, the science teacher.

Lee demonstrated the new words he had learned and the different ways he had learned to play peek-a-boo with Sharon.

Dad was really busy at work too, and when Sharon got home she would often try to get dinner organised. Lee would 'help' by washing the potatoes or getting out *all* the pots and pans ready for Sharon to use.

Dad was often tired and disgruntled when he got home from work, but he would play with Lee and read him stories while Sharon did her homework. Then she would put Lee to bed while Dad did the dishes.

It was hard work but she knew it was appreciated. Mum was grateful and when Sharon and Dad relaxed together on the couch each night after Lee was in bed, he would call her 'Princess' and tell her it was the best bacon and egg pie he had ever tasted. He would often put his arm around her, and he rubbed her aching back and shoulders, or gently stroked her face.

It was good to snuggle up beside him and she felt reassured by his strong arm. They were both tired and strained and really needed each other now.

One night as Sharon leaned against her Dad she felt his hand move onto her breast. This felt quite different and she sat very still.

For the next few nights she often felt uneasy as she felt Dad's hand move up and down her body. She wasn't really sure what to do or say. She thought she must be imagining it, or that because Dad was so tired, he didn't realise what he was doing. She wasn't sure whether to pull away or not. When she had played with herself it had been exciting and she was getting similar feelings now. Besides, if she pulled away, he couldn't help but realise where his hand was.

A few days later it was a very hot day. Sharon was wearing her shorts and she and Dad were sitting on the couch with iced coca cola as they watched her favourite TV programme. Dad had one hand on her knee. She froze as his hand started to move up her leg and start to feel about underneath her shorts. Could she really be imagining this? Dad's eyes were still on the TV but he had to know where his hand was this time. Didn't he?

Eventually she got up and went to get some more coke. Dad said he would have some too, as if nothing had happened.

The next night Sharon sat in a chair away from the couch. Her Dad said he was lonely over there by himself and seemed hurt when she was reluctant to come closer.

She kept her distance all week. He seldom looked at her or spoke to her. She started to feel really bad and the next night, wearing jeans and a long sweatshirt, went back to her old place on the couch.

This time though, when she felt his hand near her crotch, she pulled away. Her Dad held onto her and told her they needed to stick together now and comfort each other. It was hard for a man when he didn't have a woman. She had always been his little woman, but now, as he fondled her adult breasts, she was really a woman.

During the next few days Sharon felt really irritable. She was impatient with Lee. He cried a lot and then she felt really bad. She often found herself staring out of the window at school, having no idea what the teacher was talking about, or realising the rest of the class were engaged in some task for which she hadn't even heard the instructions.

The effort of putting on a happy front for Mum was exhausting. She would maintain it until she got out of the door and then feel herself crumple.

She stopped spending time with Dad at nights. She would mutter something about having homework to do (which was not entirely an excuse since she was getting so far behind at school), and escape to her bedroom. She and Dad found it hard to look at each other these days and her skin often prickled when he came close. She knew though, that his eyes followed her when she wasn't looking. She felt guilty for pushing him away. She could understand his need for comfort. She needed some too.

When Mum came home things became easier again. She still needed a lot of rest but it was a relief not to have to visit each day and Lee became full of smiles again.

Sharon forgot about what had happened between her and Dad. He wasn't around so much anyway and when he was, they didn't seem to have much to say to each other.

The difficulty was that it was impossible to maintain the smiles and jokes she had managed when visiting the hospital. Sharon found herself snapping back at the least little thing, or refusing to answer at all, and on occasions bursting into fits of rage. Her mother couldn't understand the changes in her. Nor could Sharon.

At the end of term when her report came home all her grades were down and every teacher had written remarks like 'disappointing', 'Sharon has the ability to do better', and 'more application needed'.

Her parents weren't angry. They understood how difficult it must be for Sharon to do as well as usual when she had had the extra burden of having to look after Lee and Dad. They felt the school holidays would give her a new lease of life.

Unfortunately this did not seem to be the case. Sharon felt unwell a lot of the time and often didn't get out of bed until after midday. The doctor was called but didn't seem to know what was wrong with her.

Partway through the second term, Sharon's class watched a video about incest. A girl talked about her father having intercourse with her. He was now in prison. She had been very tearful as she had spoken about the feelings she had. Sharon had wanted to get up and leave, but she felt riveted to her seat.

For days the video kept haunting her. She too had all the feelings the girl was talking about but she couldn't understand why she should feel that way when her father hadn't had intercourse with her. She thought of telling somebody, like the girl in the video had done, but that seemed impossible. She kept trying to block the thoughts out and tell herself she shouldn't be feeling what she was feeling. It didn't work. Inside, her head felt like a tumble-drier.

What would you do?
If you think Sharon should tell, turn to page 25.
If you think Sharon shouldn't tell, turn to page 27.

She hadn't intended to spill the beans, least of all to Mum. It just happened one day when she was already feeling upset. Mum had criticised her behaviour toward Dad and before she knew it Sharon said far more than she ever intended to. She stood horror-struck afterwards, holding her hand over her mouth, but it was too late. Mum looked horror-struck too, like a TV character who has been made to freeze. The silence and stillness seemed to go on for ever until, suddenly, Mum turned and left the room.

Afterwards, she was able to say to Sharon how bad she felt about doing that. At the time it had been impossible to deal with something she was unable to grasp.

Sharon, left standing alone, felt numb. She realised she desperately wanted Mum to hold her and tell her it was okay. She wasn't sure how long she stood completely motionless, but suddenly she felt the need to move, to try to shake off this awful abandoned feeling that had completely taken her over.

When she returned home hours later after blindly walking street after street, Mum and Dad were sitting at the table. She could tell Mum had been crying and Dad was pale and quiet.

The atmosphere in the house was strained for days. Mum was angry. Dad kept saying everyone was making a big deal out of nothing. This made Mum angrier still and eventually she and Sharon and Lee moved out.

Sharon was really upset about their separation. Lots of her friends' parents were divorced but she never thought it would happen to her parents. She felt it was all her fault.

Before the separation agreement could go before the court her parents were directed to get some counselling. Mum returned home to say that the counsellor said that he needed to inform the Child Protection Team about what had happened and it was likely they would decide Sharon's Dad should be prosecuted.

In the end, Mum was given custody of Sharon, which meant she was the person responsible for looking after her. Dad was not sent to prison, but was only allowed to visit every second weekend in the presence of a social worker provided Sharon wanted to see him. The court also recommended therapy for all the family members.

Sharon met regularly with a counsellor to talk about what had happened to her and how she felt about it. Sometimes it was very hard, but talking with someone who seemed to understand was helpful.

One day, Sharon's counsellor suggested that she attended a group with other teenagers who had been sexually abused. She was really scared about going and to begin with felt she didn't belong. Everyone, except her, had been forced to have intercourse. She discovered though, that other people were describing exactly the same feelings she had, and this was really reassuring.

The whole family attended family sessions. At first this was difficult too. Although they talked about lots of things apart from sex, Sharon felt embarrassed whenever they got onto that subject. There were other difficult things too – like the time her Dad had cried. She had never seen him cry before. She felt really bad and wished she had never said anything so he wouldn't have to go through this.

However, Dad explained it had been a relief to be able to cry. He had been feeling really bad anyway and if Sharon hadn't told he might have gone further one day. He was responsible for what had happened, not her, but she was the one that had made it possible for them all to get help.

Best of all, however, Mum and Dad eventually decided to get back together. They had some therapy together, to deal with the feelings they had about each other, and to try to get the difficulties sorted out so that their marriage would work out this time.

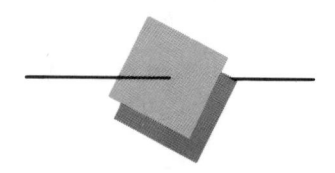

There was no way she could tell. What was there to tell anyway? It would be silly to make a fuss just because her Dad had touched her. If it had been something really important maybe she could have told.

Mum was better than she had been for a long time. It would be unthinkable to tell her about this. She might get sick again. She might even have to go back into hospital. Dad would be upset too. He hadn't really meant anything.

At the end of the spring term Sharon's report card was worse than ever. Her parents still weren't angry though. She had taken a lot of days off sick and they understood that this had made it hard to keep up.

What was worrying though was that no one knew what was wrong with her. She had had all kinds of tests but the doctor still hadn't been able to find anything. She often found it hard to concentrate. In the summer term this added to the difficulties she had. Her mind wandered one day when she was riding her bike and she crashed into a parked car. She needed stitches in her head and broke one arm.

When she went back to get the stitches out she and the doctor talked about the number of accidents and illnesses she'd had recently. He wondered if there was anything she was worried about. Sharon said it just seemed to be an unlucky year for her.

Back home, however, she realised it wasn't just to do with bad luck. She had been feeling so miserable lately it was hard to keep going at all. She often just went through the motions without concentrating. She wondered if she should tell her mother.

What would you do?
If you think Sharon should tell, turn to page 25.
If you think she shouldn't tell, read on.

Telling seemed impossible. It was such a long time ago now. It seemed ridiculous to keep dwelling on something that had happened months ago. Besides, end-of-year exams were approaching, and Sharon just had to do better this time.

School never did get much better but Sharon found other things to interest her. She started a record collection, looked after the family pets and often the neighbours' pets as well, and babysat two full nights a week.

Keeping busy kept her mind occupied. Sometimes being alone was difficult, but having records or the radio playing helped and she made sure she was really tired before she went to bed. Gradually she managed to push the thoughts about her father to the back of her mind.

Sharon married when she was 20. She had met Nigel at the youth club. He wasn't like the other boys she had known. He wasn't into being a macho man and she felt he really needed her as much as she needed him.

The trouble was, every time they had sex, she hated it. As soon as Nigel touched her, she would feel herself stiffen and pull away. She found herself thinking of all kinds of ways to get to bed before him or after him so she wouldn't have to have sex that night. She felt really bad about herself. In movies and books sex was always so exciting. There must be something wrong with her.

Nigel was understanding but she knew it was difficult for him too. She tried harder to like it but it never worked. Instead, she would lie in bed and wish it were over. Keeping busy didn't seem to work any more. Everything seemed like too much effort. She wished she could stay in bed all day. Sometimes she even wished she could go to sleep at night and never wake up in the morning.

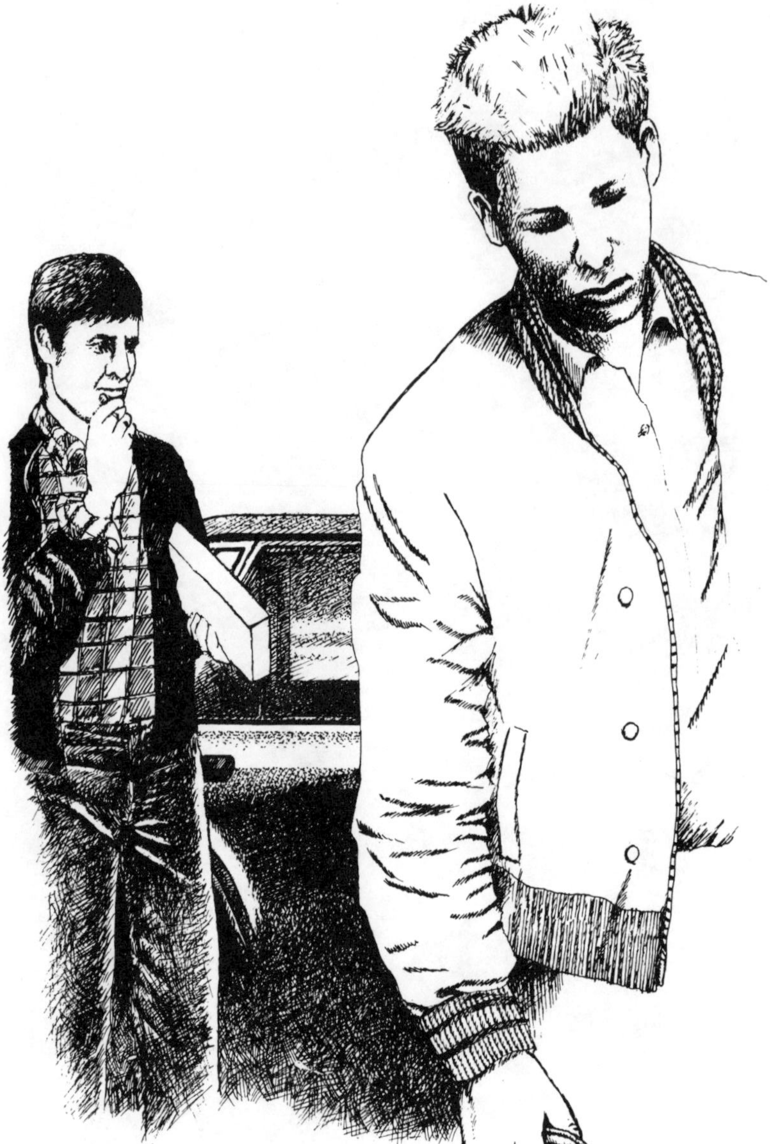

Christopher

Christopher's parents were Dutch. They had emigrated when they were first married before they had children. Life was easier here than in Holland where jobs were hard to get. The Bruyns had friends who had come out before them and they had read their letters eagerly. Hearing of the good wages to be earned and how owning your own home and car was something everyone did here, it seemed the ideal place to raise a family.

It proved to be as good as they had heard. Jens was a carpenter and had a job within a week of arriving. Maria went to work in a factory. Bringing in two wages meant they could start saving for a house straight away. They also helped Maria's sister, Lena, to come out two years later. Lena arrived when Maria was pregnant with her first child.

Jens and Maria worked hard providing for their growing family. They bought a house in the outer suburbs where there was plenty of space. Their family had grown now to three children: Mark, Karen, and then Christopher.

The Bruyns had a large circle of friends who were mainly Dutch, but also included people like Lena's new husband, Bill, who was Australian. Christopher really enjoyed the times when his parents and friends gathered together – particularly when they had barbeques on Sundays. There would always be loads of kids to play with and lots of attention from the adults. Often they would play cricket and Christopher always made sure he was on his Uncle Bill's side because he was a really good batsman.

Christopher admired the way his uncle could play sports so well and felt really honoured when Bill would give him some special cricket coaching.

When Christopher was 13 he started to become aware of his sexuality. This was a time of great change for him. He felt really good about it at times. It meant he was becoming a man. He would no longer be a little boy. He had already started to grow hairs under his arms and around his penis.

There were times though when it was really embarrassing. He would get erections at the most awkward times. Quite often it would happen in Mrs Franklin's class and it was as if she would know when he had an erection because she always chose these times to ask him to come to the front of the class to write on the board or read aloud, and he felt sure that everyone was watching his crotch.

At other times though, when it was not so public, he could find a pleasure in his own body. Christopher really enjoyed having long baths and examining the changes of his body, which seemed to happen daily. It felt so good to lie in the warm soapy water and masturbate.

Developing sexuality was a change happening in other boys Christopher was friends with too. They talked about sexual urges quite a lot and they began to experiment with giving each other pleasure as well. Christopher always had the sense that sexual play with other boys was not something he should really be doing but this added to the excitement and wasn't it just a game anyway?

Christopher was changing in other ways as well. He began to feel uncomfortable when his Mum or Dad gave him a hug or wanted to give him a goodnight kiss. It reminded him of his sexuality and that would make him feel embarrassed.

There were other important things happening in Christopher's life at this time. He was practising his cricket with determination and his Uncle Bill said he would probably make the school team with some help. Bill and Lena hadn't had any children of their own and Bill spent a lot of time at the Bruyn's home playing with the children and Christopher was his favourite. Bill often said how he wished he had children and told Christopher that he thought of him as his own son.

So despite his occasional discomfort with his uncle's attention it seemed understandable to Christopher when Bill wanted a hug. After all he must be really lonely with just him and Aunt Lena living on their own – besides, his uncle did so many things for Chris, like buying him a new cricket bat, that he felt he owed Bill something.

Christopher's feelings of discomfort continued but he kept telling himself he was just being silly. One Saturday afternoon he was around at Uncle Bill's place watching sport on TV. They were sitting together on the couch and it was one of those embarrassing times when he got an erection for no reason. He crossed his legs and moved away a little so his uncle would not see it but Bill put his arm around him and pulled him close. Chris tried to concentrate on the TV but Bill's hand was on his leg now, gently stroking. Then it was moving up until it was on Chris's penis and he was rubbing it up and down through his shorts. Chris wanted to tell him to stop. He was so embarrassed and his erection wouldn't go away. Bill kept saying 'You like that, don't you?', and how could he say he didn't when his penis stayed erect?

Bill took Chris's hand and put it on his own penis. Chris was shocked to find his uncle had his pants undone and he rubbed himself up and down with Chris's hand. The turmoil Christopher felt was awful, his stomach was doing somersaults, but his body was frozen to the couch. He couldn't say anything for a long time until the sound of Aunt Lena shutting the back door gave him the chance to break away.

The upset Christopher felt continued for a long time. He was confused by the two different feelings he had: the awful cold feeling he had every time he thought of his uncle or was touched by him, and the sense that he still owed his uncle something for all the presents and coaching he had given him.

Bill kept paying Christopher lots of attention over the

next few months, and he would often set it up so he would be alone with him. Christopher gave himself a hard time for letting it go this far. It seemed as if things were right out of his control now and had become too difficult to stop.

But then Bill went even further and made Christopher lie down while he put his penis in Chris's anus. It really hurt, the pain was terrible, and he found he was bleeding afterwards. He thought he was going to die. Chris felt like he was on a speeding train with a madman at the wheel. He just wanted it all to stop so he could get off safely.

He had begun to feel really down. He wasn't interested in playing cricket any more. It made him feel worse to see all his friends so happy and full of energy. He only felt sad and heavy and started to spend a lot of time on his own. He didn't seem to have much to say to people any more.

He would often spend the whole weekend at home staring at the TV while the rest of his family were busy doing things. Christopher's Mum and Dad noticed the change in him and tried really hard to find out what was making him so sad and quiet, but the thought of telling them seemed impossible. What would they think of him? They probably wouldn't believe it anyway. He hardly believed it was happening himself. Besides, he felt so guilty, wasn't it his fault that he had let it go this far?

But he did want it to stop, somehow. Sometimes when his parents were out he found he could make the awful feelings stop with some of the sleeping pills from the medicine cabinet or some whisky. But when he woke up the feelings were there again!

What would you do?
If you think Christopher should tell, turn to page 37.
If you think he shouldn't, turn to page 35.

Christopher felt as if he was in a deep black hole and there was no escaping. His uncle kept at him. Once, he got up the courage to tell Bill he wasn't going to have sex with him anymore. What happened next took Chris by surprise. His uncle started to cry and pleaded with him not to stop. He said that he loved him and wouldn't have anything to live for if Chris stopped 'loving' him.

Christopher felt he was even deeper in the black hole. He felt guilty that he had made Bill cry, and now felt responsible for looking after him. If he did stop, would his uncle kill himself? Chris wasn't sure, but if he did it would be his fault!

There seemed no way out. Christopher began to drink more of his parents' whisky. If he couldn't stop the runaway train, then at least he could blot out his feelings of desperation, aloneness, and sadness. It didn't work any better than before though. The minute he woke up the feelings would flood back over him.

One evening when his parents were out he took some of the sleeping pills and drank a whole bottle of wine. This time when he woke up he was in hospital. There were tubes running into his arm and he was connected up to a machine. His parents were there and a doctor as well. The doctor said that Christopher had tried to commit suicide. Christopher glanced at his parents, they were pale and looked really tired. His mother was crying and his Dad kept saying in a soft voice, 'Why Chris, why?'

Chris felt tears in his own eyes. He wished he was dead, he felt so guilty. It seemed that now he had hurt his parents as well. Again he wondered whether he should tell them.

He was discharged from hospital the next day. His parents picked him up and took him home. The atmosphere there was heavy and sad. His brother and sister didn't know what to say. His parents sat with him for hours trying to help him talk about what it was that had caused him to take the pills.

The doctor at the hospital had arranged for him to see a

psychiatrist that week. Perhaps the doctor thought that he was crazy. Christopher wondered if he might be. When he saw the psychiatrist they talked about how Chris's interest in school and sport had gradually dropped off in the last year. The doctor asked Chris if there was anything that had happened that had made him unhappy. Chris was tempted to tell but wondered whether he could. He still felt it was all his fault.

Later at home with his parents he thought again of telling. They looked so worried and tired and concerned for him.

What would you do?
If you think Chris should tell, turn to page 39.
If you think Chris shouldn't, then turn to page 48.

It seemed that no matter what he did, drinking whisky or taking pills, the awful feeling wouldn't go away.

On Saturday afternoon he was sitting in the kitchen with his mother. She was just scooping the last of the chocolate cake mix into the pan when the phone rang.

'Chris, get that will you – oh! You never answer the phone,' she continued angrily when he made no move.

Christopher was staring at the table as Mrs Bruyn reached across for the phone. He thought to himself that she was right, he didn't ever answer the phone these days. He never knew whether it would be his uncle or not. He dreaded the thought of having to talk to him. But he was suddenly brought back from his thoughts by the sound of his mother's words.

'Yes Bill, I will send him around with it straight away, bye – that was Bill, he wants you . . .' Her voice trailed off as she hung up and turned to look at Chris.

The cold sickly feeling in his stomach was threatening to reach his mouth and he quickly put his hand up to stop it.

'Chris, are you alright?' His mother had noticed how pale he had suddenly become.

Chris could feel the sickness rising in his body and the tears in his eyes. But when he took his hand away from his mouth it wasn't sickness that came rushing out, but fear and anger.

'I won't. I hate him. I hate him. I hate him . . .' he cried. It was as if all the stored up feelings came rushing out at once. Chris was crying like he had never cried before. It felt as if he was falling apart.

But his mother was holding him in her arms and he felt safe enough there to let the pain and sadness come tumbling around him.

He didn't know how long they had been there, but a quietness came over him, and he realised that he and his mother were sitting on the floor. She was holding him tightly in her arms and gently rocking.

'Chris, Chris, what is the matter? I have never heard you say that about your uncle before.'

His mother didn't understand what was happening, but she could see that something was really upsetting Chris and it was connected with Bill.

'He's – he's hurt me.'

'How has he hurt you, Chris?' Mrs Bruyn was still puzzled, but could tell by Chris's voice that it was serious.

Chris felt lost for words. How could he tell his mother about the horrible things that had happened to him? But it seemed that having made it this far he had to keep going. The warmth of his mother's body so close gave him courage.

'He made me do things to him and he did things to me. Dirty things.' The words seemed to fall from his mouth. Chris felt really awful and embarrassed but it was a relief to let go of the secret.

His mother was shocked and confused. She felt she needed some help with this and called her husband in from the back yard. Together they helped Chris to tell about what had happened between his uncle and him over the last two years. Chris said how guilty he felt, as if it was his fault that it had happened, and how this was what had stopped him from telling before. His parents said they could understand how difficult it was for Chris and to his surprise they said they did not think it was his fault. They said they thought that Bill, as an adult, was the one who should have known better and was responsible.

Chris's father and mother were both furious with Bill. Mr Bruyn wanted to go around and confront him. Maria was afraid though that her husband would be so angry that he might hit him. So after discussing what they should do, they decided that it would be better to report it to the police.

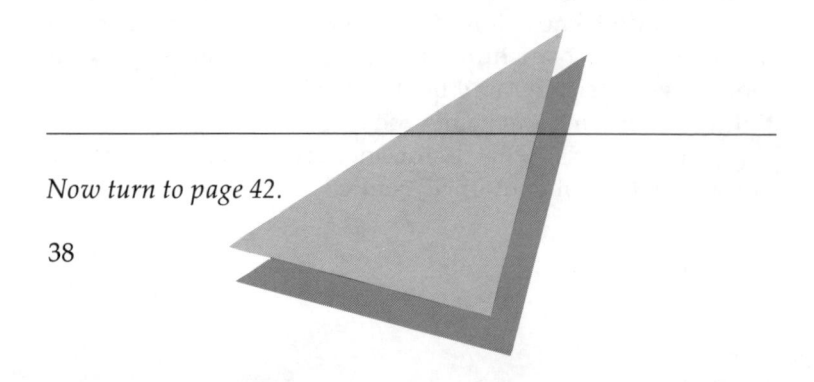

Now turn to page 42.

Chris felt sad and desperate. Carrying around this secret was like trying to hide a load of bricks under his coat. It was heavy work and difficult to keep hidden. Every now and again a brick would drop out and Chris would have to scramble to get it back out of sight before anyone saw it.

But it was tiring and he wanted someone, some adult who was strong enough, to take the load off him. It would be so good to be a teenager again. It seemed as if that part of him had been lost somewhere.

Chris could feel the load he carried as he sat outside Dr McGuire's office the next week. He wondered how strong Dr McGuire was. He wanted to share his load and it seemed safer talking to someone outside the family. That way if it was too heavy for other people to handle at least his family wouldn't be hurt by it.

But what if he couldn't cope with it and told his family anyway? It seemed really risky and Chris wondered how he might test out Dr McGuire's strength. Could he trust him not to tell his family?

'Come in, Chris.' Chris was startled out of his thoughts by the doctor's sudden appearance. Inside the office Chris felt uneasy. How much could he trust this man? There was something about him though. It was funny, Chris thought, he seemed a bit like his mother. Dr McGuire wanted to talk about feelings and was concerned about Chris and when Chris said he was sad he didn't change the subject, he even wanted to know more.

Chris continued to see Dr McGuire every week for several months. Each time he tested him out a little more, like turning up late several times to see if he got sick of him. But Dr McGuire always seemed pleased to see him and wanted to know how he had been since the last time they had met.

One day when they were talking Chris said that he didn't have a girlfriend.

'Have you ever had a sexual experience with a girl?' asked Dr McGuire.

The words 'with a girl' jumped out at Chris. He

stumbled around for an answer. It felt like a brick had dropped out.

'Ah – ah – not with a girl,' he blurted out.

'It is common for teenage boys to have sexual experiences with other boys,' added Dr McGuire.

The brick was lying there but the doctor seemed not to see it. Chris felt in a real dilemma. He could conceal it again now if he really wanted.

'Are you worried about being gay, Chris?' continued Dr McGuire.

Chris could feel the load begin to tumble. 'I have had sex with my uncle . . .'

It came like an avalanche. He said more than he ever thought he would when this moment came. He told Dr McGuire about how his uncle didn't have any children and had always paid Chris lots of attention. It had all seemed so reasonable at first. He had felt he owed his uncle something. But then Bill had said he would kill himself if Chris didn't continue to have sex with him. It seemed as if it was his fault that it had all started.

Chris was surprised by Dr McGuire's response to him spilling the beans. He didn't say it was his fault or pretend it was unimportant. In fact he took it very seriously. But when Chris asked him not to tell anyone he was worried by Dr McGuire's response.

'Chris, this is very serious. This is a criminal offence your uncle has committed. Besides, I don't think keeping this a secret is going to do you or anyone any good. If we try to sweep this under the carpet it won't go away and we will keep tripping over it.'

'But my parents would die if they found out,' pleaded Chris.

'I am not sure they would, you know. You and I could meet with them together and I could help you explain. Would that be easier?'

Chris knew that he was probably right, he did trust him.

'How about I give them a call and we could meet tomorrow,' continued Dr McGuire.

'So soon?'

'It is important that we deal with this, Chris,' Dr McGuire insisted.

'Well, I suppose so . . .'

'In the meantime, will you have any trouble with your uncle?' enquired Dr McGuire.

'No. He hasn't been around for ages,' replied Chris.

Dr McGuire then called Chris's parents and arranged for them to meet the next morning.

Chris found it really difficult the next day when they all met in Dr McGuire's office. He felt relieved though that Dr McGuire was there and helped so much, and his parents really did seem to understand. His Dad got extremely angry with Bill and wanted to go around and confront him. Dr McGuire said that was the job of the police and they needed to report what had happened to them.

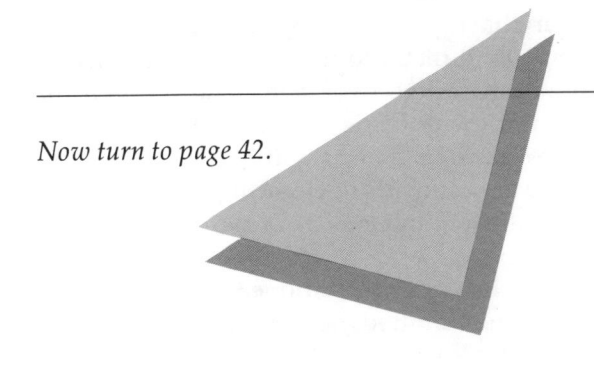

Now turn to page 42.

Chris's stomach felt like it was knotted up as he and his parents walked into the Police Station, but he felt safe with his mother and father there to talk for him. The sergeant took the three of them into a room down the corridor after Mr Bruyn explained what they had come to report.

They didn't have to wait very long before two detectives came in and introduced themselves. First they wanted to hear from Chris. His parents were allowed to stay though. Chris felt awful having to go through the whole thing again with two strangers, but his parents helped him and the police took it very seriously.

Then Chris's parents had to make a statement as well. They found it difficult too and they kept saying how guilty they felt for not having noticed it was happening.

The police then said Chris's parents could take him home but they weren't to have any contact with his uncle until he had been interviewed by the police.

It was several days before the police contacted the Bruyns again. Chris had begun to wonder if they were going to do anything about it – perhaps they hadn't believed him after all. But they had been to talk to his uncle, who had admitted to sexually assaulting Chris. They had arrested him, but he was going to be let out on bail until the court case, on the condition that he had no contact with Chris.

It was two months before the case came to court. Chris found it really scary having to be in the same court room as his uncle. It was really difficult to have to repeat the whole story again, but the two detectives had gone through the story a couple of times with Chris before the hearing so he knew what sort of questions he was going to be asked. The most difficult part was seeing his uncle sitting there with his head hung down. Bill wouldn't look at Chris, and Chris was glad he didn't.

After his uncle had been questioned by the lawyers and the judge and he admitted he was guilty, the judge adjourned the court for some time. It seemed to take ages, but then he called everyone in again and announced that he found Chris's uncle guilty and sentenced him to two years in prison.

After they left the court and Chris was sitting in the back seat of the car on his way home, he felt a strange mixture of things. Two years in prison seemed a long time and he almost felt sorry for Bill. But at the same time he thought two years was not enough compared with how hurt he felt. Part of him said it should have been ten years – even twenty.

Things didn't get immediately better for Chris. There were times when he still felt really low. He didn't want to go out much in case he met anyone he knew because they were bound to know what had happened – particularly since it had gone to court. People always talked, he knew they would, and he knew what they would say about him.

His parents were still really worried about him being so sad and not wanting to go out. They asked their doctor what they could do. He advised them that Chris should see a psychotherapist. He said that Chris would have a lot of feelings about what had happened to him and that although it was good that they could talk with Chris about it (and they should continue to do so), he would get quite a bit out of talking to a therapist who had had a lot of experience in helping teenagers who had been sexually abused.

So Chris began to see a child psychotherapist once a week. It took a long time before Chris began to feel differently about himself. He continued to see his therapist for almost a year.

But what seemed to change things for him after that time was joining a therapy group where he met others who had been sexually abused. Most of them were girls, but there was another boy there too. 'Maybe I am not so alone in the world after all,' he thought.

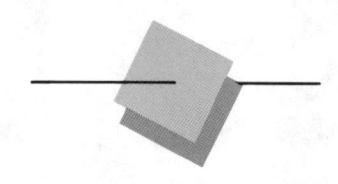

Robyn came to visit on Thursdays each week. Chris had been feeling really down all weekend. He had come to the decision that he had to tell someone about the sexual abuse. Since he had spent every day of the last 16 years thinking about it, keeping on pretending it was unimportant was pointless.

It seemed an endless wait until Thursday. Chris wondered and worried how he might tell Robyn. He got even less sleep than usual that week. His decision to tell, however, was strong and he felt certain that this was something he had to do.

Thursday arrived. Chris had been unable to stay asleep and had been up since 4 o'clock that morning. He had sat in the kitchen drinking cups of tea and going over what he might say. Robyn usually arrived at 10 o'clock so at 9.30 he went out onto the verandah to wait.

Chris could feel his heart pounding as the hospital car turned the corner and came into view. Faint doubts started to creep into his head as Robyn came up the path. He knew he had to do something quickly or he wouldn't go through with this.

'Hello Ch–' began Robyn, but she was cut short by Chris.

'There is something I have to tell you Robyn.' Chris blurted the words out before they could escape back inside.

'Are you alright Chris?' asked Robyn.

'There is just something I have to tell you,' repeated Chris. He felt there was no going back now.

'Okay, shall we go inside?' asked Robyn.

In the security of his room Chris told Robyn about what had happened to him as a child. It was hard. At times Chris could not say anything and tears streamed down his face. Robyn sat and listened as Chris continued his story. He told her about how he felt so guilty and responsible for the whole occurrence, how he felt he must be mad, and how that had snowballed until everyone else thought he was mad as well.

Chris found it was such a relief to be able to tell someone. He was surprised by Robyn who sat and listened and seemed to take him so seriously. That was something he hadn't experienced before. He wondered if she really did believe him, or was she just being a psychiatric nurse and saying all the 'right' things to make him feel good. So at one point he stopped and . . .

'You do believe me, don't you?' asked Chris.

'Yes, I do Chris,' replied Robyn. 'I do because I have worked with a lot of people who have been sexually abused and I know how serious it is, and how its effects can go on for ever and may destroy some people unless something is done and they get some help to deal with it.'

She really does believe me, thought Chris. He almost laughed, he felt so happy. At last someone who believes me!

Chris talked to Robyn about his past a lot over the next six months. He began to feel quite different about himself, confident and more interested in what was going on around him.

One day while Chris and Robyn were talking she suggested he might like to come to a therapy group for incest survivors that she was involved in running. At first Chris's reaction was a definite 'NO'. How could he talk about his abuse to anyone else? It would be impossible to talk to others. What good could it possibly do anyway? Besides, this was something Robyn and he shared. Talking about it in his room with Robyn was one thing, but exposing it outside of here was something else.

Robyn suggested the group again several weeks later. Chris was interested to know what went on in the groups. Did they really sit around and go over and over their stories each week as he imagined? Robyn explained that yes, they did sometimes talk about the original experience, but that they talked about other things as well. Often what the group spent most time on was talking about what was happening to them now and how they might be able to make that different. This surprised Chris, it was not what he imagined happened at all.

Chris thought about the group a lot that week. What kept coming back into his thoughts was that there were others out there who'd had similar experiences to his own. Even other men, not just women as he had thought at first. Maybe he could go along and see what it was like just once.

As Chris packed his things together he looked about at the room he had lived in at the halfway house for so long, and smiled. It had been eight months since he had gone to his first group. Things had happened so rapidly since then. He found it almost impossible to imagine how he had found the confidence to leave the halfway house and move into his own flat.

He closed the door to the house and, suitcase in hand, strode out through the front gate.

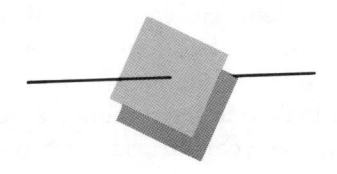

It felt too awful to even think about the things that had happened with his uncle. To tell anyone about it seemed impossible.

Chris felt he had blown it years ago when he first let Bill spend so much time with him and his biggest mistake had been to let his uncle hug him. It seemed as if he had started it all and now he had to pay for it.

At times Chris wondered if he had ever wanted his uncle to do these things to him. After all he hadn't made him stop. Maybe he was gay? But he didn't really like having sex with his uncle. What if there was something about him that made men want to have sex with him? Perhaps there was something wrong in his head, perhaps he was cracked or crazy.

The argument went on and on in his head. The part that said it was his fault and that he was bad and worthless got stronger and stronger. Sometimes he would catch himself answering it back out loud. He knew that talking to yourself was weird but since he thought he must be crazy anyway it didn't seem to matter.

The trouble was though, that the talking inside his head got pretty loud sometimes. It stopped him sleeping and occasionally he would realise people had been talking to him and he hadn't heard them. He wondered if they had been talking about him. Once he had almost been run over by a car while crossing the street. He had been so busy listening to himself he hadn't looked to see if there was any traffic.

Over the next few years Chris kept using pills and alcohol to stop the arguments, but they wouldn't go away completely. Other teenagers used to call him 'crazy Chris' and 'the looney'. Chris hated it when others gave him a hard time but he had dropped out of school by the time he was 15 and it was easier when he could just stay at home in his room.

He had seen several psychiatrists over the last couple of years, but all that had happened was they had given him more pills to take. There was talk of him going to stay in a hospital now though. All Chris wanted was to stay in his room, but what did it matter what he wanted? They would get their way anyhow. It seemed to Chris that people had always made him do what they wanted.

So Chris went to hospital. There was no point struggling, they always won. The staff there were no different. They told him what to do and when to do it. Once you were in there and the door was locked the staff just did what they wanted and said 'It is all for your own good' or 'You will like this, Chris'. But Chris didn't believe that.

By the time Chris was 25 he had been in and out of the hospital many times. He felt like he was on a merry-go-round with other people at the controls. Every day was just a blur. He had been on medication for so long he was not sure what he was supposed to think or feel anymore. He was so tired of it all, he wanted to just go to sleep and not wake up. He thought about saving up the pills the nurses gave him and taking them all at once.

The only thing that he looked forward to each week was seeing Robyn, his community nurse. She would visit him at the halfway house where he lived. She would even come to see him when he was in hospital. Chris felt that she was the only person in the world who cared enough to listen to him. He had thought from time to time about telling her about what it had been like all those years ago when he was a teenager. But it had happened so long ago.

Chris has got to the point where he now has three choices. Each one has far-reaching effects. None is easy. Some cannot be reversed once put into action. Choose carefully!

Would you choose to tell the nurse about what had happened to you as a teenager? If so, turn to page 45.
Would you choose to kill yourself by taking the pills? If so, turn to page 16.
Would you choose to do nothing and remain a patient in the psychiatric hospital for . . . years?
If so, you will have to write this story yourself!

49

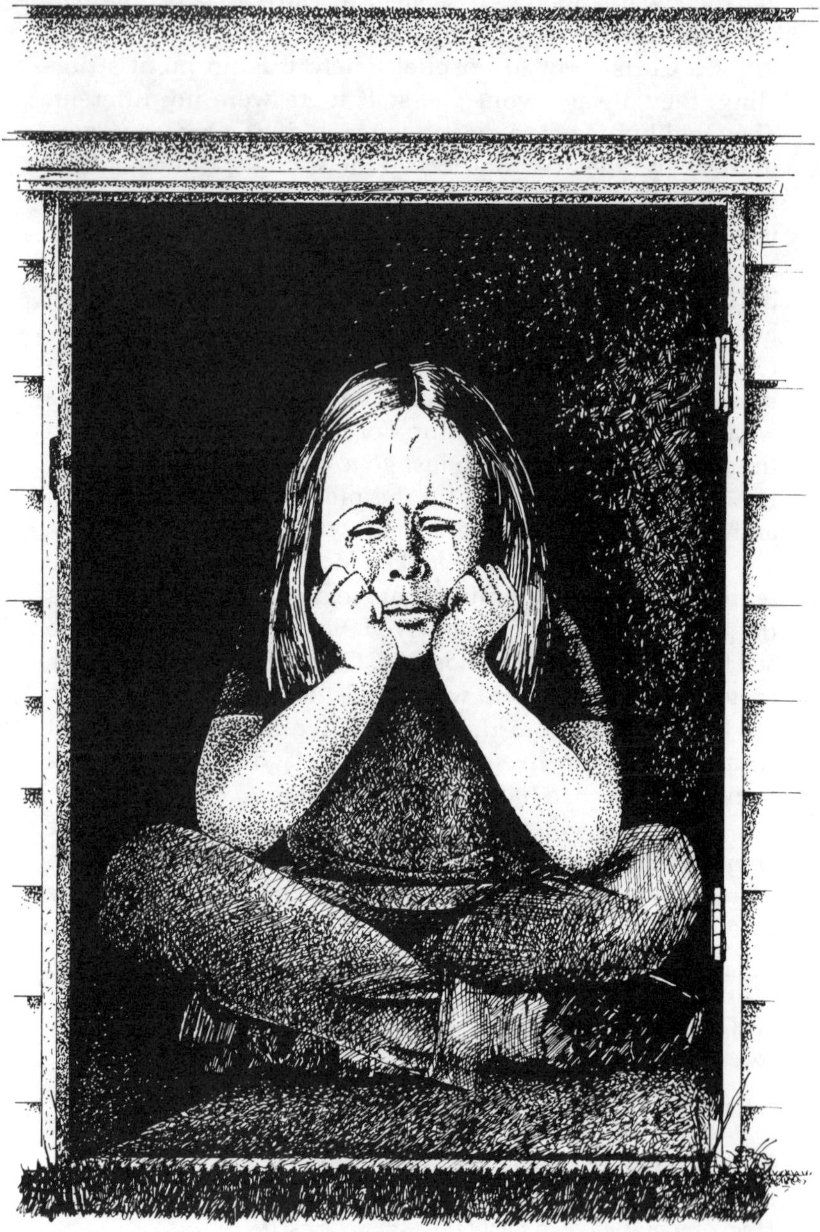

Natasha

Natasha's birth was a really big event. Mum said that four boys was enough. It was a shock to find herself pregnant again five years later, but having a girl made it all worthwhile.

It was difficult for Natasha's mother to look after the new baby, as well as four growing energetic boys and her husband. She always seemed to be doing several things at once, but when the boys were at school and there was just she and Natasha she had more time to enjoy looking after her. However, Natasha didn't seem to stay a baby for long. Once she could walk she got into all kinds of mischief and Mum had to be on her toes. It was also hard for her to grow up with four brothers who always played so rough. Sometimes she would cry when she was left out, but when they let her join in, she often got hurt. They always said she was a cry-baby and Mum said if she wanted to play with them she would have to learn to be tougher.

When Natasha started school, Peter and Nick made a big fuss about having to take her, but were secretly proud. Natasha couldn't get there fast enough. For as long as she could remember her brothers had always gone off to school, first to the local infant school with only two classes that was near their home, and then by bus to the school in town where Jason and Darren now went. She couldn't wait to get home to tell Mum all about it. The novelty didn't wear off and each day after school, when Mum was cooking dinner, she would sit in the kitchen and tell her all about it.

Dad was home more often now. There was less work around for him to do at this time of the year. He spent hours in his shed out the back, and in the evenings and weekends Natasha would go out and help Dad fix the lawnmower and work on the car. She would sit on Dad's knee while they listened to the races, and he would give her sips of his beer.

It was fun to be in the shed. There were lots of old cars to hide in, and tyres to roll and all sorts of junk to play with. Her brother Darren was old enough to have his own car now. She would often try to help him but she seemed to only get in the way with Darren. He would yell at her to get away and she would run back to Dad. She could snuggle up against her Dad and his big arms would make her feel very safe. Sometimes when she was snuggling up to him he used to put his hands in her pants and play with her vagina with his big fingers. One day he took her pants right off, unzipped his fly and rubbed his penis up against her. He went funny in the face, like it was hurting him, but he didn't stop. When he did she felt all wet and sticky on her legs. He told her this was a new way they could have fun together but they had to keep it a secret. It was something special for only the two of them to know about.

School continued to be a place Natasha really liked to be. She liked the work in the classroom but best of all she liked to be outside. She was the best runner out of her whole year at school. She also knew that she was even better than some of the older pupils. She liked her teacher, Mrs Anderson, and often stayed and helped after school to try and please her.

The secret between her and Dad continued. She wasn't sure why he didn't want her to tell, but he often reminded her that it was their secret.

Once when he was rubbing up against her, he started to force his enormous penis inside her vagina. She said it hurt. He told her it would hurt for only a little while, but it wasn't just a little while. It hurt for a really long time. She cried and cried.

Afterwards he said he was sorry and held her till she

stopped crying, and again reminded her that it was their secret. Natasha didn't feel like telling anyway. All she wanted to do was hide. Her best hiding place was at the school but that was too far away, and it hurt to walk. She knew she couldn't possibly climb her favourite tree, so she crept into the little wardrobe in her bedroom.

Natasha stopped going out to the shed after that. She didn't think it was a very nice place any more. Sometimes when she was hiding she would hear her Dad call, but she pretended she didn't hear.

Peter was chasing her around the yard one day when she fell and scraped her knee. Dad came and picked her up and carried her into the shed to put a bandage on it. He gave her a cuddle to make it better. He said it had been such a long time since he had had cuddles from her and he wanted a big one. Natasha struggled as Dad forced her to have sex again but was unable to fight against his weight crushing down on her. It hurt just as much as the last time and she said she didn't want to do this any more. Dad said it was really nice for him and since she hadn't told about it he would make it nice for her too. He would buy her some new roller-skates and maybe even the horse she had always wanted.

Back in her hiding place, Natasha thought about what a big and scary world it was out there. She seemed to be in a world of giants. She often felt as if she had been trampled under their feet. Night times were scary too. Monsters kept coming into her room and she would have to run and run to get away but in spite of going through the motions of running, she often didn't seem to be able to move. She would go from one place to another to hide but just as she thought she was safe they would jump out, smiling their wicked smiles, showing their huge yellow teeth, and stretching their awful claws out towards her.

She often woke in the night and wanted to go to the toilet. The house was dark and enormous and made horrible creaking noises. The end of the passage seemed miles away. Sometimes she would creep along it shaking all over, her heart pounding so loudly she knew the monsters would be able to hear it and know she was there. At other times she had wet the bed because she couldn't bring herself to get up. Her mother got really angry when this happened but that only made it worse. Natasha would lie in bed knowing Mum would be angry, but if she got up the monsters would probably grab her before Mum got to her anyway.

Everything seemed so big and overwhelming. During the next few years she spent hours in her cosy, warm wardrobe. It was small, only a little bit bigger than her, and it was the only place in the world where she filled up the space.

It was dark in there, and to begin with that had scared her and so after a while she started to take a torch in with her. She knew the light would keep the monsters away. She didn't really like the dolls and teddies her Dad kept buying her but sometimes when she really wanted some company, she would take them in too.

One time, when Dad was having sex with her in the shed, Darren came in. He stopped suddenly. He moved to the other end of the shed behind his car, but he didn't go right away. He didn't say anything to her but she knew he and Dad were talking afterwards. A few days later Darren called her to come and hold down the brake pedal for him while he did something in the engine. As soon as she was in the car he told her to move over because he was getting in too. He knew what she and Dad had been doing and it wasn't fair for Dad to keep her all to himself. Natasha tried to get away, but Darren held onto her. She said she would tell. He told her she'd better not or he would give her the biggest hiding she had ever had.

She didn't tell, but it didn't seem long before Jason and Nick knew as well. They wanted to have a turn with her too and made all kinds of threats about what they would do if she didn't agree.

The family were all at the races on New Year's Day. It was the first time for ages that they had all gone out together – usually the boys went out with their friends and Mum and

Dad and Natasha hardly ever went anywhere these days. No one had made any money and they were all feeling disgruntled. When it was time to go home Natasha started to get in the car but all of a sudden she felt a volcano well up inside her. She knew there was no way she was going to get in the car. The volcano erupted in shrieks and yells. 'I won't, I won't. I am not getting in. You can't make me.'

The family told her not to be so stupid. It had been a long day, they were tired and wanted to get home. Natasha screamed louder than ever and when Darren and Jason tried to force her to get in, she bit and kicked and scratched. She screamed at them on the way home, 'You are always hurting me, I am sick of being hurt, I hate you, I have had enough.' Mum told her not to be so silly and Dad, Darren, Jason, and Nick winked at each other and told her to stop all the imagining she was doing. It was playing tricks with her mind. Only Peter stayed silent. Natasha sobbed the rest of the way home.

The volcano didn't go away. Sometimes it even erupted at school. Often something quite little caused the eruption. Natasha knew she was being unreasonable but then explosions just seemed to take her over. She spent a lot of time being sent outside the classroom door and having to stay in after school. Being kept in didn't always seem like a punishment though. In spite of the fact that Ms Shaw gave her extra work to do, she was often kind to her and Natasha felt good inside when she praised her work. She was trying not to think about next year when she would be at secondary school and wouldn't see Ms Shaw any longer.

Eruptions became more frequent at home as well. One day she heard Mum telling Auntie Norma, 'I never thought I would have a problem child like Tash.' Dad talked about 'Tash's little fits' and Darren and Jason and Nick made comments like 'danger zone area, approach with caution' or 'beware of missiles'. She felt like firing missiles and often did. She hurled abuse at them and sometimes objects as well. Once she threw a full milk bottle at Jason. It smashed into the wall right beside him. Fragments of glass got embedded in his face. Mum came running and screamed at her how hateful and horrible she was. Natasha spent hours cleaning the floor and wall. She kept cutting herself as she picked through the mess of glass and blood and tears.

Mostly though, she was really scared of the boys. They kept threatening what they would do if she ever told. She knew they weren't kidding. They hurt her enough as it was.

The night before she started secondary school Nick had kept coming into her room. She had had a horrible nightmare and had woken in the early hours of the morning dripping with sweat and shaking all over. In the morning when she was already feeling uptight about school, Darren and Jason had started giving her a hard time.

She left the house carrying the present Dad had given her, a new backpack, but feeling like she was carrying backpacks of aggro from everyone in the family. Even when she got to her new school she didn't seem able to put down the backpacks of aggro and right from the first day she got a reputation for being a trouble-maker.

The new school was huge and unfamiliar. She wanted to be somewhere where she filled up the space. All day she felt like a dwarf in a land of giants and thought about her old school and her space in the wardrobe. She hadn't heard the teacher speaking to her, and by the time she realised it was her he was talking to, he had become really impatient. 'What did you say?' she asked. This seemed to really annoy him. It felt like he was on her back as well and that was definitely one load too many. The volcano overtook her. She snapped back at him and then stormed out of the classroom before the volcano had a chance to cause major destruction.

Having a reputation was difficult. Some kids tested her out to see how tough she really was and others didn't want to have anything to do with her. Teachers expected her to be tough, so often jumped on her before she had even done anything. It meant she constantly had to be angry and defiant. Although it was often a relief to get rid of some of her anger, she felt worse and worse inside.

There was a group of kids though that she fitted in

with. Only tough kids 'gained admission' to this group, and Natasha managed to become a member within weeks of being at school. Together they got their own back by hounding other kids, upsetting teachers by disrupting their classes, and refusing to obey when they were given punishments or sent to the detention room.

They went round together after school as well. They were good at embarrassing people who walked past. They managed to get off with things from shops without the shopkeeper being 100% sure of whether to accuse them or not, and succeeded in getting teachers who thought they were smoking to retreat feeling confused and embarrassed. Soon they were experimenting with glue sniffing.

After a while they met up with some teenagers who had left school. They were old enough to be able to get alcohol and they also knew ways to get drugs. Down by the river after school they would spend hours lying in the long grass, drinking and smoking. This meant that Natasha often missed the only bus home.

Nick and Jason had their own cars now too, and sometimes they would give her a ride. 'One good turn deserves another, they would say.' At other times she didn't go home at all and often didn't go to school either. This caused enormous fights but she didn't care.

Being with her friends often felt just as unsafe as being at home. Sometimes fights broke out, especially fights over girls. Bludge had needed 30 stitches when Rat had attacked him with a broken bottle for making a pass at his girl. Taking drugs and glue sniffing was often scary but at least her friends cared about her. Once she had taken pills and had a lot to drink and been very very sick. She knew she looked and smelled awful, but they hadn't gone away. When she had got over thinking she was going to die she had been able to appreciate the way they had looked after her. She felt she had found somewhere to belong, a place where she fitted.

The first time one of the boys tried to kiss her she wanted to throw up. She tried to pull away. He told her not to be such a tease. She had been holding out all this time but he knew she really wanted him. Sex with him was just the same as with Dad and her brothers, but she had got used to blocking it out by now. Having sex with Pox wasn't what she wanted, but it was nice to have someone around who cared about her.

By now Natasha was away from school more than she was there. One day the Education Welfare Officer called round to see her parents. Mum was furious with him for checking up and interfering, and furious with Natasha for causing the family's privacy to be disrupted. The arguments got worse and worse every time Natasha didn't arrive home. Her parents started to lock her in her room. This stopped Natasha getting out but it didn't stop Dad and Jason and Darren and Nick getting in. Natasha started barricading the door with the furniture but this made them more determined still and Natasha more angry than ever.

One night when she was really furious she put her fist through the window. She cut herself badly getting out but she didn't care. She decided she was never going to be imprisoned again.

Being on the run wasn't easy. It was hard to find places to stay. Some nights were spent in the open, sometimes there was not enough food and when there were no drugs to relieve the cold and hunger, Natasha often felt miserable. Having Rat to look after her helped though. She felt uncomfortable whenever she saw Pox, but, after all, he hadn't struggled too hard to keep her once Rat had made his intentions clear. Belonging to Rat felt safe. No one ever tried to pinch Rat's girlfriends. Rat was so big no one even challenged him. When he put his arms around her Natasha felt like she fitted in, and felt safe. She didn't like having sex with Rat but maybe it didn't matter. She already felt used and dirty. It was like wiping your dirty hands on a towel. The first time you really spoiled it, but after it had been used time and time again, what did a few more marks matter. Besides, it was what she was used to doing – trading her body, in order to get some caring. It wasn't the kind of caring she really wanted but it seemed the only kind she could get and some was better than none.

The day the police caught up with them she knew she hadn't been as careful at avoiding them as she usually was. Rat, knowing how practised she was at getting away with things, couldn't believe she hadn't done it deliberately. She wasn't altogether sure herself.

When her parents drove away from the girls' centre, she felt amazingly lost and lonely. She hadn't really expected them to welcome her back home with open arms, but although she tried not to let herself hope too much, some part of her felt that when they saw how miserable and hurt she was, they would take her back. She felt she was drowning in a sea of loneliness. As far ahead as she could see, in whatever direction she looked, there was nothing but an enormous unfamiliar sea. She felt no bigger than a piece of seaweed being tossed about at the will of the ocean. Waves washed over her, battering her, and then there were periods of calm. Cold, empty, unending calm.

That feeling lasted most of the first week. Natasha didn't even think about her volcano. It seemed to be extinct. She was really surprised when it suddenly erupted and she shrieked and swore at one of the staff members. Afterwards she felt bad, but also relieved in a funny kind of way. Overwhelming anger was really scary, but anything was better than the nothingness of the past week. During the calm times the staff tried to talk to Natasha. They wondered about her anger, but as soon as they started asking her questions, she instantly became angry and they gave up. She hated people prying and questioning her. She had never given anything away when her family had tried to check up on her, and she certainly wasn't going to do so now.

She hated the staff. She fought with the girls too, but at times when the staff were being a real pain, the girls stuck up for each other. Often groups of them went on the run together. When they were caught, it always meant being locked in the secure room which she hated, but at the time the freedom seemed worth it.

At other times she was locked up on her own for several hours because she had got out of control. Staff members would come to bring her meals. They would often try to talk to her about what had made her so angry, but Natasha said nothing.

One day, when Ms Latta came back to collect her plate, she didn't go away immediately, but just sat with Natasha. It felt kind of nice, but after a while Natasha snapped, 'Why don't you say something?' Ms Latta said, 'I wasn't sure you wanted to talk.' Natasha said, 'I don't', and turned her back. Ms Latta said, 'It is okay with me if you don't. When I am really hurt I don't always feel like talking either.'

Natasha was startled. She suddenly wanted to cry. She didn't think anyone could possibly have known about the hurt. How could Ms Latta know when she had worked so hard to hide it? Tears sprang up in her eyes. She had an overwhelming urge to share the pain with Ms Latta, but as soon as she let it surface she became really scared. The hurt was too big to bring out into the open. It would overwhelm her and probably Ms Latta as well. She quickly blinked back the tears and hoped Ms Latta hadn't noticed. 'What hurt?' she said.

It was several more months before Natasha was able to really talk about the hurt. She started to a few times, but got scared. She quickly became angry. That helped to stop the hurt taking her over. It also kept Ms Latta at a distance and that was important because letting her get too close would mean she might not be able to control the urge to talk about the hurt.

When it did happen Natasha hadn't meant to say so much. It was just after her parents had visited. They talked about how good things were at home. Natasha felt sure things must have changed because she wasn't there. Sometimes they phoned and gave hints about missing her and wanting her back but whenever they came to visit, they made it clear that she was too much trouble and they couldn't go through all that again. Natasha wasn't all that sure she even wanted to go home now, but whenever they left the sea of loneliness seemed to take her over.

She was still feeling this way when Ms Latta came along and all of a sudden she found a flood of words and tears pouring out all over the place. Ms Latta put her arm around her shoulders and after the words and tears had stopped they sat that way for a long time.

Afterwards Natasha did feel very exposed and vulnerable, like a turtle without its shell. At times she really did think the hurt might overwhelm her.

During the next few days, however, Ms Latta often sought Natasha out when she was on her own. Sometimes they just sat together but at other times Natasha did manage to talk about how awful she felt – misunderstood, rejected, and unwanted. She could understand how her family felt though. It wasn't surprising they didn't like her. She didn't like herself either.

Gradually she stopped feeling so overwhelmed and strangely enough Ms Latta didn't seem overwhelmed either. At first she had kept expecting her to say, 'That is enough, Tasha', or 'Pull yourself together, Tasha', or to rush off because she was busy.

She was less angry nowadays too, although at times there were still flare-ups.

She had become angry with Mr Henderson one day and had started to throw the book she was holding across the room. Mr Henderson had grabbed her and held her arm. The feeling of being pinned down was terrifying and Natasha fought like a wild cat.

Later, Ms Latta commented on how angry Natasha had been with Mr Henderson. She said she had noticed that Natasha often gave the male social workers a hard time and she had been wondering about that. 'They get up my nose,' said Natasha.

When she thought about what Ms Latta had said, she knew she was right. Some of the women staff members got up her nose too but she didn't react in quite the same way.

The more she thought about it, the more she realised she didn't like men at all. They were all the same. You could never feel safe when they were around. Once, being with Dad had felt safe. She had really trusted him and loved him but she hated what he had done to her. If you couldn't trust the man who was most supposed to look after you, there was no way you could trust other men.

She hadn't really explained this to Ms Latta. At the time, she hadn't been able to explain it to herself. She wondered if she should tell her. She wasn't sure she could. Ms Latta might tell her family she had told, and the storms would start all over again. She also wondered how it would be for Ms Latta if she knew. Natasha knew *she* couldn't cope with it, she couldn't even bear to think about what had happened. Ms Latta might not be able to cope either.

On the other hand, Ms Latta hadn't been overwhelmed when she had shared her hurt. It had felt good to know someone else understood.

What would you do?
If you think Natasha should tell, turn to page 63.
If you think Natasha shouldn't tell, turn to page 67.

'I have been thinking about what you said,' said Natasha. 'I don't like any men. It is because . . .'

There were several times when she nearly stopped herself. Although the feelings had been inside her for a long time she had never spoken the words before and they didn't feel like hers. She didn't want to look at Ms Latta but every now and then she would glance at her, wondering what she was thinking.

Things happened quickly after that. The police came and interviewed her and then went and interviewed her family. She hadn't been there, but she heard her Dad had laughed and said, 'Tasha is always making up stories.' Her mother had been shocked that Natasha would say such things. After all the trouble she had put them through the last few years, this was just too much. Besides, Natasha was always telling lies. She would say she had been kept in after school when she was really down at the river smoking and drinking. She would say her friends had given her money when she had really stolen it. With a reputation like that she was surprised the police had taken Natasha seriously at all.

Jason and Darren and Nick had laughed and pointed out that Natasha had slept with all the local boys so they supposed it was natural for her to make out she had slept with them too. Peter had said nothing.

Natasha wasn't sure whether the police believed her or not but it was decided not to prosecute her father and brothers. The police said there was no one to back up her story. In court there would be five people against one and even if the judge believed her it wouldn't be possible to convict her father and brothers because of the lack of evidence.

Natasha felt furious with her family. She wanted to kill them all. She lay in bed at night making plans as to how she could do it. When she finally got to sleep, however, she often dreamt it was them who were attacking her. She would wake in the night screaming and sobbing and later would feel so angry that they were all carrying on enjoying themselves as if nothing had happened, while she felt so awful. She didn't ever want to see any of them again.

When her mother phoned to say that Darren had hanged himself Natasha was amazed. Why had he done it? She got into endless debates with herself. Maybe she was responsible for killing him. She had been so preoccupied planning ways to do it maybe she had actually caused it to happen. But how could she? He didn't know what she had been thinking. People only killed themselves when they were unhappy, didn't they? Since she left hadn't they all been happy without her?

At the funeral she didn't want to talk to any of them. They hadn't wanted her and she now didn't want them. The girls' centre was the only family she had now.

It turned out, though, that the girls' centre wasn't going to be her family either. They had been looking for a foster family placement for her. She knew girls didn't stay on for ever but finding another family seemed like a dream. She felt shattered when they announced they had. She had only just begun to fit in here. How could she begin all over again? The staff understood her shock, but said she needed a family she could belong to for a long time, not just short term.

Fitting in with the new family wasn't easy. It meant a whole lot of changes, new rules, new ideas, new things to get used to. Natasha thought it must be hard for them as well. She couldn't believe they really wanted her. At times she tried extremely hard to fit in and to try and please them. She kept very quiet so as not to say the wrong thing and offend anyone. She made sure everyone else got what they wanted and even though that often meant she missed out it was one way she could make them like her. Sometimes when she really couldn't believe they would want her she would go on the run. If no one tried to find her then she would know she was right. They always did though, and soon there was no point in doing it any more.

There were times when she still felt bad, but she had made good friends at her new school, and there were a lot of good times in her new family as well. She also attended a group with other teenagers who had been sexually abused. To begin with she felt like chucking it in. Being there was like opening up stab wounds. That was really painful and she thought she might bleed to death.

The group was led by two therapists, a woman and a man. Natasha felt secure with the woman but she made sure she never sat near the man. She hated him from the moment she walked in. At times she felt so angry with him she wanted to leave early or to not go at all because she feared she might punch him in the face.

As the weeks went by, however, she started to feel very puzzled by him. He hadn't tried to take advantage of anyone in the group. She had been constantly rude to him and although he had sometimes got angry, he hadn't tried to hit her or hurt her. Sometimes he even said things that made her think he really understood. At first she thought he was pretending and that made her hate him more than ever but after a while she started to think maybe he *really* did understand.

She didn't believe she could ever like him, but when the group ended she found she didn't want to say goodbye to him.

Saying goodbye to the group was awful. She was sad it had ended but she knew she didn't need it any more. At first she hadn't trusted the others in the group but gradually they had shared a lot about themselves. It had been wonderful finding others who knew what she had been through and were able to really understand. Even though she wouldn't see them in the group again she knew they would remain friends.

Opening the wounds had let them heal. It had taken time and she knew the scars were still there. Now, though, she could go for days, or even weeks, without ever being aware of them.

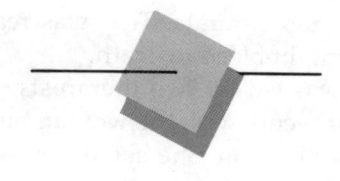

What was the point in telling? There was nothing Ms Latta could do anyway. It would only stir up more trouble and Natasha didn't need to work at that. It seemed to happen anyway without her actively going in search of it. She couldn't understand why but Ms Latta often behaved as if she liked her. Having someone like her had been like having a life belt thrown to her when she had felt she was drowning in her sea of loneliness. She knew other girls at the home had been sexually abused. It wasn't often talked about but she had heard staff members tell them not to blame themselves. It wasn't their fault.

Natasha felt sure that didn't apply to her though. Maybe if she had been abused by just one person she could believe it wasn't her fault, but being abused by four meant there had to be something about *her* that made it happen. If Ms Latta knew how dirty and awful she really was, how could she possibly go on liking her?

Besides, what was the use? When things went wrong there was no point in dwelling on them. Mum always said she made a fuss about nothing. 'You have to put things behind you and look on the bright side,' she would say. Natasha had often been puzzled about this because her parents didn't seem to be able to put her drinking and smoking and missing school behind them. They brought it up all the time.

She supposed though, that telling would be making a fuss. Considering all the other things that had happened maybe it wasn't such a big deal anyway.

Several weeks later it was decided Natasha should go back home. She felt panic-stricken. Although she had hoped and hoped her parents would say they really wanted her, going home was very scary. If she went back to her old school she would get in with her gang again and the same thing would happen all over again. If she didn't join them they would make life really difficult for her.

She felt sick every time she thought of Dad and her brothers forcing themselves on her. She would go crazy if that happened again.

Plans were going ahead though and a discharge date was being set. Natasha again thought of telling.

What would you do?
If you think Natasha should tell, turn to page 63.
If you think Natasha shouldn't tell, turn to page 69.

It was strange being back at home. When she was at the girls' centre Natasha had thought of all the things about home she missed. Now she was there it was hard to remember what they were.

She stayed well away from the shed. That didn't stop Dad and her brothers pestering her though. She would lie in bed at night waiting, dreading the sound of footsteps coming closer or the sight of the door handle moving. One or other of them almost always arrived and when they didn't she lay waiting and waiting, hoping no one would come, but unable to sleep because she knew they would. She hated it. She hated them. She felt very small and helpless when they forced themselves onto her, but in her mind she made herself powerful by dreaming of killing them. She would do it slowly. She would make them cringe and cower. Then they would beg and plead with her not to do it, just as she had had to do with them. It wouldn't do any good though. Finally she would finish them off. A bloody, gruesome, horrible death.

When she slept, however, she often dreamt it was them who were attacking her. She would wake in the night screaming and sobbing and later would feel so angry when they continued to behave as if nothing had happened and they hadn't a care in the world.

When Nick went into the shed one day he came out howling like a wild animal. The family tried to get him to say what was wrong but he couldn't stop sobbing. He tried to speak but all that came out were a lot of sounds that no one could understand. Eventually he became calm enough to make sense. Darren had hanged himself on the rafters.

The family were distressed. Natasha was amazed. Why had he done it? She got into endless debates with herself. Maybe she was responsible for killing him. She had been so preoccupied planning ways to do it, maybe she had actually caused it to happen. But how could she? He didn't know what she had been thinking. People only killed themselves when they were unhappy, didn't they? Darren always seemed very much in control to her, and not unhappy at all.

It seemed like death had overtaken all the family. Even after the funeral there was a deathly hush in the house – no sound, no movement. The tension was unbearable. Natasha had to get out. She really was drowning this time. She could feel herself being sucked under. That night she fled.

When she was found her family were furious. Didn't they have enough to worry about at the moment without her adding to their problems? Things had been fine when she was in the girls' centre. They should never have brought her back home. Darren might still be alive if she hadn't been around to stir up trouble again.

They hadn't hit her, but the words fell like blow after blow. Natasha felt beaten to a pulp. She couldn't think or feel or react. All she knew was she had to get away.

Down by the river she drank litres of beer. It didn't seem to help. She wanted to be further and further away. So far away she never came back. She persuaded her friends Rocker and Camshaft to take her in their car, as far and as fast as the Cortina could go. They took her at her word. She had never ridden so fast before. They had several near misses at sharp corners but she didn't care. What did it matter if she lived or died?

When the car plunged over the bank, Tasha felt sure this must be it. She wished it would stop rolling so she would know whether she was dead or alive.

She was surprised to discover, when she regained consciousness, that she was still alive. Surprised and somewhat disappointed. She had missed her chance to end it all.

When she came out of Intensive Care she still had several months of lying flat on her back in the Orthopaedic Ward ahead of her. She spent hours lying motionless gazing at the ceiling. She hardly knew whether it was day or night. She stopped eating and became thinner and thinner.

The hospital staff were worried about her. They sent a psychiatrist to talk to her. She didn't want to see a shrink. Dr Carmichael was really curious about Natasha. She smiled as she approached this thin little girl with dark curls who looked more like 10 than 15. Her face was tight and pinched.

She spoke in a monotone and made sure she avoided meeting Dr Carmichael's eyes. Talking to her was like trying to get information from a computer that had gone off-line. Dr Carmichael felt she was walking in a mine field. Every move had to be made cautiously. There was something about Natasha that told her if she stepped in the wrong place, an explosion could occur. In spite of this there was something about her – she couldn't quite put her finger on it – something in the way Natasha's eyes clouded over at times and the way she dug her fingernails into the palms of her hands. For whatever reason Dr Carmichael knew she wanted to stay.

Natasha felt irritated as Dr Carmichael asked her a lot of questions about her life and family and friends. She said 'yes' or 'no' to each question, and when neither of those fitted, answered in as few words as possible.

After a while she started to wonder about Dr Carmichael, but she wasn't going to give her the satisfaction of looking at her. She was puzzled that the doctor didn't seem irritated with her. Dr Carmichael's voice was soft and warm and didn't seem to change no matter how rude Natasha was.

Dr Carmichael was finding this hard work but her instincts told her to hang on. She was wondering where to step next. She knew about Darren having hung himself and that definitely seemed unsafe territory. She decided to chance it though.

'Natasha, I am wondering how close you were to your brother who killed himself?'

There was a silence, Natasha wondered what to say. She had been close – too close. That wasn't what the psychiatrist meant, though. How could she explain? She thought about telling.

What would you do?
If you think Natasha should tell, turn to page 73.
If you think Natasha shouldn't tell, turn to page 72.

Natasha could move around with the help of crutches by the time she left hospital. Her leg and hip still hurt whenever she moved. It was winter now. In the hospital it had been warm day and night, and she had not even realised the seasons were changing. Outside the wind seemed to blow right through her. She couldn't remember ever feeling so cold before. Maybe it was because she was so thin. People had kept telling her how thin she was but she hadn't agreed with them at the time.

She didn't want to go home but it was obvious there was no choice. She couldn't run away with her leg in plaster. Even if she could it would be really miserable in the winter. Besides, what did it matter? What did anything matter? It didn't even matter whether she lived or died.

The stay in hospital was the first of several for Natasha. During the following few years brushes with death became almost commonplace. She had several bad experiences with drugs and frequently overdosed and was unconscious for hours afterwards. She was involved in a head-on collision with another car which left her with a permanent back injury and scars on her face. On another occasion she misjudged a corner when she had had too much to drink. The car plunged over a bank. Natasha was thrown out and suffered severe internal injuries.

Most people were sympathetic and told her how unlucky she was. Natasha knew this wasn't so. Her theory was that she had been born bad. She deserved all this pain and suffering. She had been in the way ever since she was little. She had often caused arguments and fights. She had been angry and violent and caused a lot of distress to her parents during times she had run away, and she had been responsible for Darren's death. No, it wasn't unlucky. With a list of sins as long as hers what else could she expect? She would probably kill herself next time, or, worse still, maybe she wouldn't.

'I was close,' said Natasha. 'Too close.'

For weeks she had felt nothing. She had not laughed or smiled even when visitors tried to cheer her up. She had never been angry, even when Jason had bumped her dislocated shoulder or when the nurse had managed to turn her arm into a pin cushion in her attempts to find a vein. She had not felt sad, even when the rest of the ward had shed buckets of tears watching a heart-wrenching film on TV. Even when she had heard about the permanent back injury she hadn't cried.

She was quite unprepared for what happened next. She had no sooner spoken the words than tears poured down her face and her whole body was taken over by huge racking sobs. In the next few hours she told the psychiatrist what had happened with her Dad and her brothers. She talked about the pain, the revulsion, the disgust, the anger, and the hurt. Afterwards she felt exhausted. It was like spending months in a dark silent room and suddenly being flooded with light and sound and movement.

She had barely had time for her heartbeat to return to normal when a policewoman arrived wanting a statement from her. Natasha felt too wrung out to start all over again but Dr Carmichael said she would help, so Natasha agreed. The policewoman was pleased because they needed information from her right away. They planned to interview all the members of the family before they had any idea she had told. They felt it would be hard for Natasha to keep the secret next time the family came to visit if this wasn't dealt with right away.

The police interviewed all Natasha's family separately. She didn't hear what happened immediately, but later it became clear that they had accused her of lying and been really angry with her.

Dr Carmichael suggested they all meet together to try to sort out the different versions of what had happened. The family were reluctant to come but eventually they turned up, dragging their feet, stony faced, and strangely silent. They quickly exchanged the silence for anger, fired in sharp bursts towards Natasha, leaving her wounded and immobilised.

Dr Carmichael tried to get all the family members to talk about themselves and how they got on together, but the family seized every opportunity to return to Tasha and her failings. They went on and on about how she was always in trouble at school ('when she was there, that was') and how awful her friends were ('not that you could really describe them as friends'). They couldn't imagine what Natasha saw in them. They dragged everything up – the sniffing, the drinking, the drugs, sex with all the local boys, being so bad she had to be sent to the girls' centre. They went on and on about how they had really tried to help and how awful it had been to have Natasha away from home. There was nothing they could do though. They knew the doctor would understand that there were limits to what parents could tolerate. She could see for herself how irresponsible Natasha was. She wouldn't be top to toe in plaster if she was reliable and trustworthy.

Natasha retreated to her 'dark silent room'. She knew Dr Carmichael had tried to stick up for her but afterwards when she came to talk to her alone she wished she would go away. She wanted to stay in her 'dark silent room'.

'Forget it,' she said.

Dr Carmichael said she couldn't forget it. Natasha's father and brothers had broken the law. Their abusing Natasha had had a major effect on her life. It wasn't something either of them could forget.

However, after discussions with the police, it was decided not to prosecute. No one could back up Natasha's story and in court there would be five people against one. Even if the judge believed her it wouldn't be possible to convict her father and brothers because of the lack of evidence.

Dr Carmichael emphasised that this didn't mean she thought Natasha was telling lies. It was just that she felt putting Natasha through all the trauma of criminal court proceedings would be really difficult if there was only a slim chance of winning.

One thing was clear though. Natasha couldn't live at home again. It was important she lived somewhere where she could be safe. For this to happen Natasha still did have to go to court, not the Criminal Court, but the Children and Young Persons' Court. A social worker spoke on her behalf. She asked that Social Welfare be made responsible for Natasha since her parents had not been able to keep her safe. The judge agreed to this and when she came out of hospital Natasha went to live in a foster home.

Trying to be part of a new family is difficult and a lot can go wrong.

If you think Natasha didn't fit in, I am sure you will be able to come up with your own ending to this story.
If you think Natasha did fit in, turn to page 65.

Part TWO

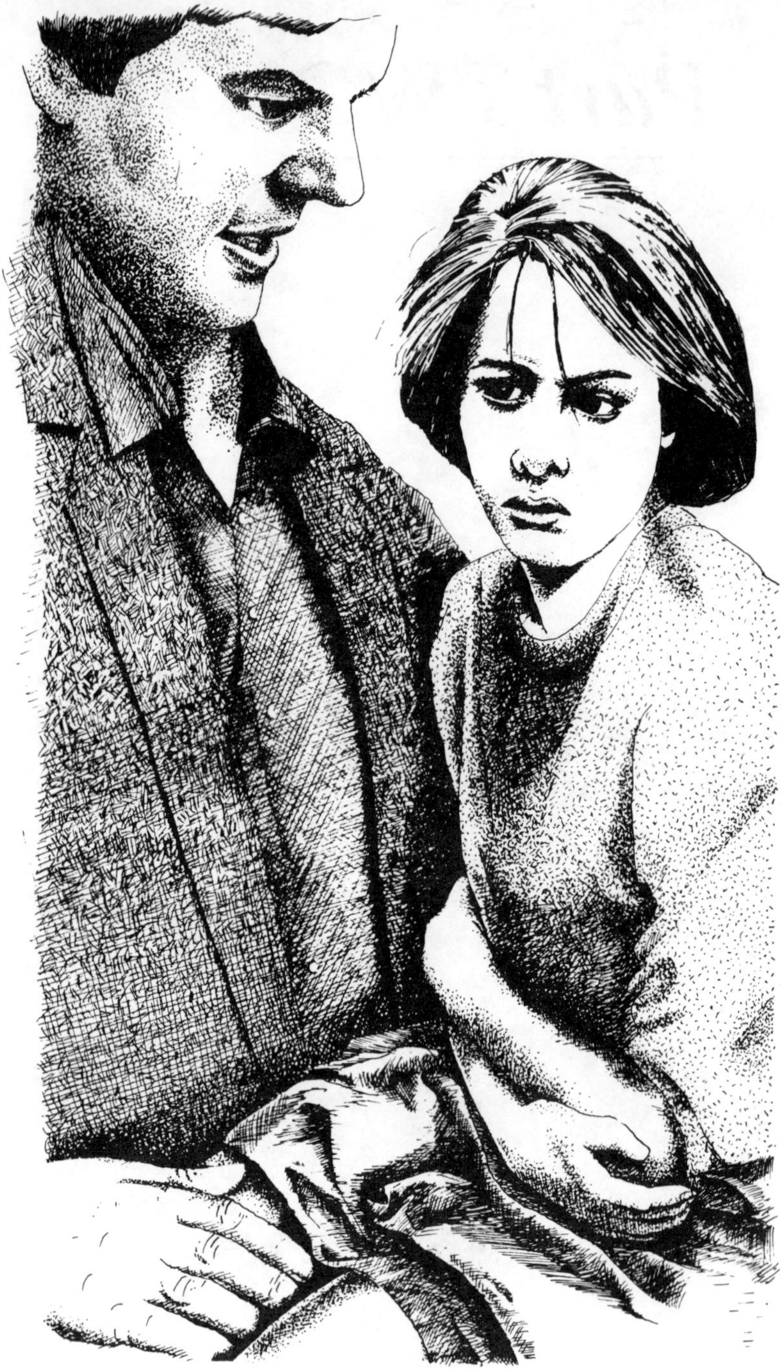

What is 'it'?

Sexual abuse is not just intercourse with your father – that is, having him put his penis in your vagina. It is also being touched in places that are uncomfortable for you – on your breasts, your vagina, or anus if you are a girl, or your penis or anus if you are a boy.

It is being made to do things you don't want to. Like having to stroke a man's penis or put it in your mouth or having to undress while he watches or being undressed by his eyes.

People who abuse can be fathers, stepfathers, Mum's boyfriend, grandfathers, uncles, close 'family friends', and brothers. Usually it is someone who is connected to the family and has some power within it.

Sometimes females are abusers too, although this does not happen as often.

Incest is an abuse of power

Sometimes it happens by force, because he is bigger and stronger than you are or he threatens to hurt you if you don't co-operate.

Sometimes it happens because he uses a kind of blackmail to get you to co-operate. He might tell you how special you are and how much he needs to use you and your body. If you refuse to co-operate he might give you a hard time for the rest of the week, or might ignore you altogether.

Sometimes it happens because he tricks you. He tells you this is what all fathers and daughters or sons do. He tells you this is 'our little secret' and if other people find out the secret will be spoiled.

Sometimes it happens because you are looking after someone else who is important to you. He may threaten to do it with your little sister or say he will beat up your mother.

He may also lead you to believe that it is your mother's fault that he is needing to have sex with you. He may give you hard luck stories about her not loving him. He is likely to be very convincing, and you might believe him and agree to have sex with him so he will leave your mother in peace, or so he will stay living with her and not leave her all alone again.

Sometimes it happens because you think he loves you and it seems likely he is the only person in the world who does. When you are feeling very needy you are much more likely to be persuaded by his attentions. That makes it easier for him to take advantage of you and get what he wants.

The most untalked about subject in the world

In Britain 12% of girls and 8% of boys are sexually abused by the time they are 16. Some are abused by strangers, but most are abused by members of their own family or a close family 'friend'. Usually the abuse takes place in the victim's own home.

For girls, this means that if you attend a single sex school, it is likely that 3 or 4 girls in your class have been sexually abused.

For boys, this means that if you attend a single sex school, it is likely that 2 or 3 boys in your class have been sexually abused.

If you attend a mixed school, it is likely that 3 people in your class have been sexually abused – or 1 girl per netball team; or 1 boy per cricket team.

If so many young people have been abused, how come you have never heard anyone talk about it? There are a lot of reasons why, but these are some of the most important ones:

▷ A lot of people want to pretend it doesn't exist because believing it would shatter the illusion that men always take care of us, provide for us, and protect us from harm. Believing in this illusion is what makes us feel safe.

▷ A lot of people want to pretend it doesn't exist because of the fear that they might have to get involved. Getting involved might mean they would feel uncomfortable, they might have to state their opinion, and stand by it; they would run the risk of people getting angry or upset with them and they fear they would get 'tainted' with the messy situation.

▷ A lot of people have difficulty talking about bodies and sex. They either don't talk about them at all, or make jokes, or turn sex into some kind of competition.

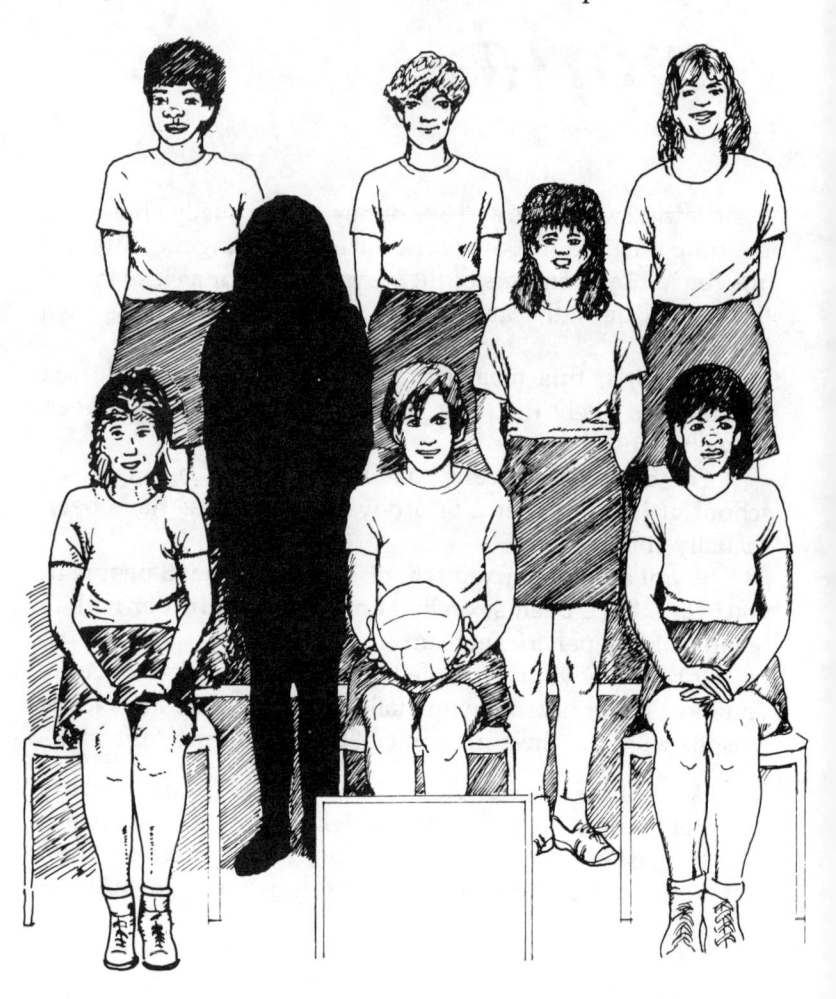

Why did he do it?

At first the question seems to be, 'Why did he want to have sex with me?' Being sexually abused, however, is not really about sex at all.

The man who abused you is someone who had more 'power' than you. He was an adult, or at least older, bigger, stronger, more knowledgeable.

Often men believe it is their right to be the 'ruler' in the family, not just over the children, but also over the adult females as well. One way they do this is by violent means like beating them up. Other ways, which are less violent but just as effective, are not letting the women or children have paid jobs or contacts outside the family, not giving the family money to live on, or simply not doing any work within the family (such as not doing any chores or looking after children).

This is just an extension of how our society is built. Men at the top and women and children at the bottom. The men have been able to stay at the top for a very long time by standing on top of everyone else to stop them becoming powerful.

Traditionally a man has had enormous power over a woman. This had included the 'right' to physically control her and have sex with her whenever he liked, despite what she wanted. He could tell his wife and children what to do, just as if he owned them. So a lot of men believe it is their 'right' to do what they want with their children, even have sex with them.

IT IS NOT THEIR RIGHT THOUGH, IT NEVER HAS BEEN AND NEVER WILL BE.

How can a man physically and sexually abuse children and not feel guilty, bad or anything?

Often he does have these feelings, but these are too uncomfortable for him, so he either tries to 'bury' them, or he finds ways of justifying his actions in his own mind.

Most of the time, however, he can't allow himself to feel for others when his shaky male pride is so threatened. He is, in fact, feeling very weak himself, but one way he makes himself feel more powerful is to put down someone who is younger and weaker. He is like an eggshell that has had its insides taken out. He is fragile and likely to shatter at any moment, so he makes himself strong by shattering someone else.

He has probably never felt properly cared for, nor does he know how to care. He expects women to look after him but he has never had to look after anyone else. He has been taught, perhaps by watching his father, that it is his right to be looked after and not to have to give in return. So he can't truly love someone else and feel for them. He believes he and his feelings are the most important and everyone else is less important.

All this is not to excuse him for the hurt and damage he has done to you. THERE IS NO EXCUSE. As an adult it is his responsibility, his alone, and he has to accept the consequences of his actions.

Why did she let him?

Maybe she doesn't know or maybe, at times, she had her suspicions, but there are numerous reasons why she may not be able to let herself believe them, particularly if the person who abused you is her partner.

If she is someone who doesn't feel very good about herself she may need him to make her feel better. She may feel that she will 'go under' if she has to cope with the world alone so the only way she can stay safe is to stay with him. (This is especially likely if she has had previous marriages or relationships that have not worked out.) This makes it almost impossible for her to believe it.

She is likely to feel undesirable and unwanted. Her man has chosen you instead of her. That is very hurtful. She is likely to feel extremely angry with him for rejecting her, hurting you, and having secrets that she wasn't part of.

She is likely to feel guilty. She may tell herself she should have chosen a better partner, she should have been more aware of what was happening, she shouldn't have gone out so often, or she should have protected you better.

These feelings may overwhelm your mother and the only way she may be able to manage them is to pretend that it isn't happening. Even if you tell her, not believing you means that she doesn't have to believe it herself.

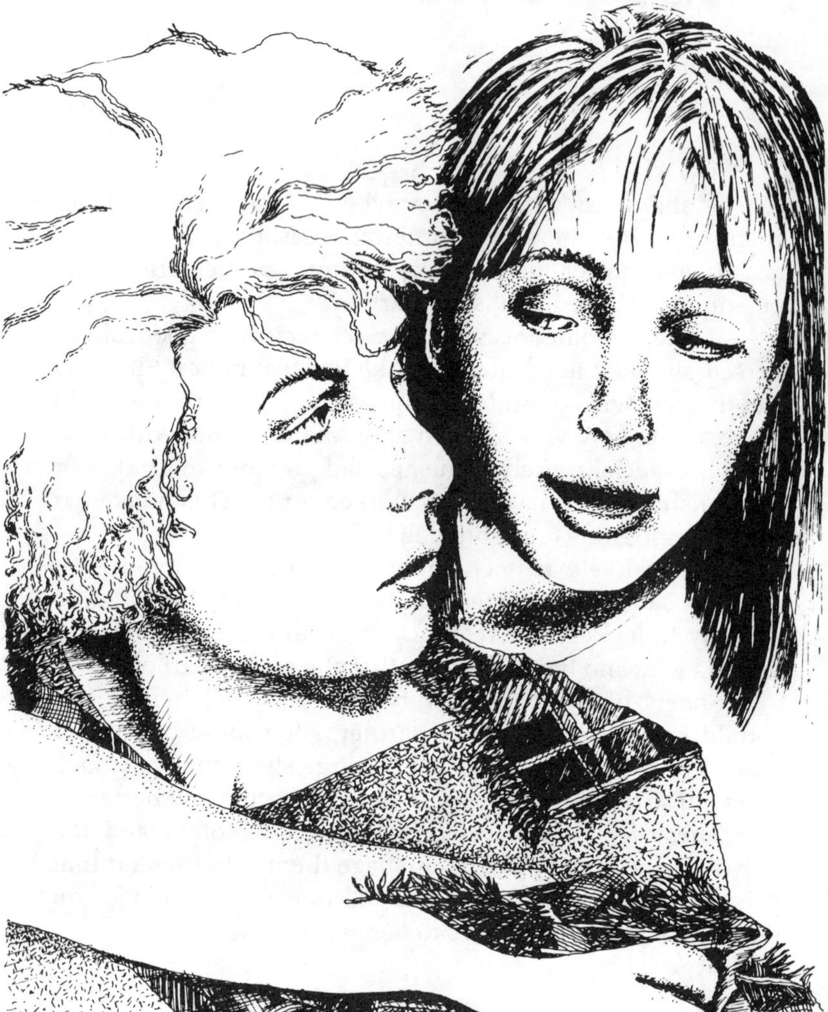

Feelings you might have

It is just not worth trusting people

'I used to dream of going to live with another family but that is impossible because no one could like or care for me. It is pretty hard believing anyone any more. I am always let down. That is why I hardly ever take chances.'

When you have been used, let down and betrayed by someone close to you you expect other people to behave in a similar way. Having been badly hurt, it is really natural to try to protect yourself from ever being hurt again. It is likely you do this by not letting people get close to you. You may achieve this by being 'a tough kid'. The more fragile and hurt you feel on the inside the tougher you will behave on the outside. You may be distant with people – polite but cool.

You may keep yourself to yourself.

You will have trouble when people touch you – especially *some* people.

Mistrusting people can work as a protection. It can also mean you miss out on getting fun, warmth, closeness, and caring.

No one in the world believes me

'I feel so angry, there is this screaming going on inside me, but it can't get out because my mouth has been so tightly shut for years nothing can escape.'

Keeping even a little secret is a hard thing to do. Keeping a big secret, like being sexually abused, is an enormous task. It often feels like a huge weight that you have to carry around with you all the time. Although that is an enormous strain when you have carried it for years, you may get so used to it being there, that it feels normal.

Trying to share the load is a scary thing to do because you can never be really sure what will happen. For this reason you may have tried to give out hints rather than come right out and say it. That way you can always take it back again if you have to. The trouble with doing it this way is that people don't always pick up the hints and you don't get any reward for the risks you have taken, but instead feel as if nobody thought what you were saying was worthwhile.

Coming right out and saying can start you on the road to recovery if the person you tell believes you and does the right thing. If this doesn't happen though, you can feel even worse than before. When families don't want to hear something that might damage them they often behave like a venus flytrap plant that has been poked, closing so tightly that it becomes stifling to be inside. People often behave angrily when they feel threatened. To be angry with the person who abused you would mean they would have to believe it was true. That might be just too threatening so they may get angry with *you* instead.

Another way families behave when they feel threatened is to pretend it is not true. In order to really believe this they have to work at keeping on saying it – things like:

▷ 'How could you say such things?'
▷ 'It is all in your mind.'

D-

Alone in the world

'I feel like a freak. I must be the only one in the world that this has happened to.'

▷ 'Your imagination runs away with you.'
▷ 'Don't be stupid.'

When this is said to you often enough, you really start to wonder whether you did imagine it. Even though the abuse is continuing and you know it is real, when you are flooded with doubts from your family it becomes difficult to distinguish what is real and what isn't.

Telling someone outside your family can be just as difficult, particularly when people know the person who is abusing you as a good bloke, or an elder at church, or manager of a company, or squash champion, or community leader, or Mr Nice Guy. People may find it hard to believe that someone they know and like would behave this way.

Something else that may happen when you tell is that people believe you but may act like it really isn't that important. They say things like:

▷ 'Don't make such a big deal about it.'
▷ 'You should be over it by now.'
▷ 'You are making a fuss about nothing.'
▷ 'We don't want the family pride to be destroyed by this so you will just have to forget it.'
▷ 'It was wrong of him but you have just got to put it behind you.'

Or they *do* things like:

▷ Your mother continues to sleep with him even though she knows.
▷ Your mother still decides to marry him even though she knows.
▷ Social Services know but leave your sister living with him alone.

▷ The teachers know and send you to a counsellor who sees you once a week but doesn't even ask to see your family, so you end up feeling even more as if there is something wrong with *you*.

Reactions like this are extremely confusing because people are *saying* that they believe you but are *acting* as if they don't.

If you have already tried to tell and this has happened you will know what it is like. If you haven't told though, it is important to remember that this doesn't have to happen. Make sure you read the tips about 'telling' in the section on page 125.

Having to carry the secret of the sexual abuse around is going to make you feel cut off from others. You have been given responsibility for something that most teenagers aren't, and this is going to make you feel different.

Also, because you may be feeling guilty, responsible, and bad about yourself and about being raped and abused it is not the sort of thing that is going to be easy to talk about to others. More often than not others probably haven't wanted to know. They might find the thought of adult men having sex with children and teenagers too shocking to consider – or perhaps they don't want to know because it reminds them of something painful from their own childhood.

What happens when you feel so bad about yourself is that you start imagining other people are also thinking bad things about you. You think they are talking about you, criticising your appearance, and knowing what you are thinking even though you are trying to make your face completely blank. You probably think people know you have been sexually abused just by looking at you.

Checking out whether this is real or not is often too scary. Although they are probably not thinking anything like you imagine they are thinking, there is always the chance that you might be right. So what happens is that you go on thinking you know what they are thinking, until you are completely convinced you are right.

Whether it is one or all of these reasons, or others,

probably what you are feeling is terribly alone. Perhaps that you must be the only one in the world that this has happened to, as if you are not normal. How could you know there are so many girls, women, boys, and men out there that have been used, abused, and raped by the very people who were supposed to take care of them and protect them?

These feelings of aloneness don't just happen on Sundays or when there is no one around – but all the time, and are to do with feeling alone from *everyone*. They are about not having a friend you can talk to about what is *really* going on inside you. And perhaps not having a family, a mother, or father, or sister you can really be *together* with. There are the endless days of sitting alone looking out of the window, watching things pass you by like pictures on a TV, part of a different reality, a different world.

Worth nothing to no one

Feeling worthless, worth nothing to no one, is something that people who have been sexually abused say they often feel. They say that they feel as if they have been used and are now dirty and soiled – and how could anyone like them now? You might think: if he did this to me, and he was supposed to protect and care for me, look what he did. I didn't mean anything to him.

Maybe you have been thrown out of your family and if no one there, not even your mother, thought you were worth saving . . . then it is extremely hard to think of yourself as being worth much. So you feel used and abused. You feel all the good parts have been taken away, and there is nothing left that anyone could like. Only the rotten and dirty parts, the guilt, the shame, and the pain, and who would want those?

It is not surprising that you should have some of these feelings. After all, you have been abused and misused, and he has taken away a precious part of you that you didn't want to give away.

Although you might feel battered inside and robbed of the good parts, there is still something valuable there. No one can take that away from you.

Shame

Shame is the feeling you have when you know you have a rotten part inside you and you would just want to die if anyone got to find out about it. It is like saying something stupid in class and being humiliated and ridiculed by your teacher in front of everyone, or wetting your pants in a public place, or being told that you have taken more than your fair share *again*, and now everyone else has to go without.

It is the kind of feeling you have when you feel 10 cm high or the kind of feeling you would have if you were the only naked person at a party. You feel very exposed and you imagine everyone is staring at you and secretly smiling or thinking how awful you are or perhaps pitying you. It is the kind of feeling that makes you want to squirm.

Usually, really shameful things are not spoken about by anyone. Since sexual abuse is seldom talked about this makes it seem like something too shameful to expose to the light of day. Even though it is something that is done *to* you *by* someone else, the fact that you were there makes you feel like the shame belongs with you. You start telling yourself things like: 'I didn't have to go round to his house' or 'I didn't have to sit on his lap' or 'at my age I should have been able to stop it'.

Having sexual experiences when you are young means you have a lot of knowledge that most other kids don't have. This increases your chances of somehow saying or doing the wrong things with other kids and other adults. Right now, as you are reading this, you may remember times you have done this. That squirmy, 'closing off' feeling might be taking you over without your even inviting it to.

When feelings of shame take over a big part of you, you start to work very hard at avoiding people so you don't have to cope with the feeling of being exposed. If they get too close they might see right inside you and know about the rotten bits. There are numerous ways you might stop this happening:

▷ Never looking people in the eye or alternatively looking so hard that you force them to look away. Either way there is no eye contact.
▷ Avoiding people altogether by crossing the road, hiding behind the clothes racks in shops, or staying at home so you can't be seen at all.
▷ Starting to imagine what people are thinking, getting the awful squirmy feeling, and becoming immobilised and completely blank and numb.

▷ Becoming increasingly anxious, maybe blushing, biting your nails, pulling your hair, sitting on the edge of your chair, talking a lot, or not talking at all.
▷ Getting angry or hostile to keep people from coming any closer.
▷ Keeping yourself under perfect control so they (and you) won't be able to get past the perfection and really see 'inside'.

You have possibly become very good at a whole lot of these and the more successful you get the less able you will be to find out what others are *really thinking*. It may well be that people aren't thinking awful things about you or sniggering behind your back, but when you feel shame, imagining they are is something you do to yourself all the time. What you are really doing is turning *your* eyes inward and watching yourself.

Each time you do this you start giving yourself the messages that have been given to you – 'I'm bad, I'm stupid, I'm selfish, I'm hopeless, I'm dirty'.

A lot of messages though, haven't been given to you in words and there are no words to describe the feeling you have – the awful squirmy feeling blocks everything else out.

The combination of it and the abusive messages you give yourself eventually make you believe that this is the way you really are.

I feel like I have to keep this rage inside me for ever

You may feel puzzled reading this heading. Often people who have been sexually abused say they don't feel angry. There are several reasons for this.

If you have been unsure of how much people in your family love you, you have probably tried to do things to show them how lovable you are. If you have spent years putting on a pleasant front and burying angry feelings, it is likely that you have got so good at it that even you don't know you are angry.

Often loving and hating feelings are really mixed up. The person who abused you may also be the only person who showed you any love. How could you hate the only person who loved you?

It may be that it has been really unsafe for you to be angry. In some families, arguments, or expressions of anger, always end up in violence. Standing up to people, answering back, letting them know how you feel, may have meant that you have got hurt. You may have been threatened that if you told about the abuse, awful things would happen to you.

If you hang around for ages waiting for your best friend to turn up as you had arranged and discover he/she has forgotten, or you discover he/she has been telling others things about you that you had shared as a special secret, it is likely you will feel really angry.

When you have been sexually abused, you have been let down and cheated in a much bigger way. Cheated of your childhood and betrayed by one of the people who is closest to you. It is likely that you will feel so angry you will want to rage and smash and hurt and damage and kill.

Angry feelings this strong are really scary. People often feel like a boiling pressure-cooker. If they take the lid off and let out even a little burst of anger, the rest will come pouring after and completely take them over. It isn't surprising that people keep the lid firmly on.

Sometimes you can find 'safe' ways to let out little bursts – kicking the cat, slamming the door, pinching the next door neighbour's mail, giving a 'wimpy' classmate a hard time.

Alternatively you may get back at the person it is really intended for, in safe ways – putting cloves in his apple pie when you know he hates cloves, mislaying his new record, leaving the cupboard door open in the hope he will hit his head.

Keeping the lid on a pressure-cooker full of anger is

hard work. You may have to consciously work at it. Sometimes your muscles get tense and sore. You get pins and needles and cramp, stomach aches and headaches.

When you are asleep, however, your body and mind can't work so hard. Often anger appears in dreams in all kinds of ways.

The other important thing that happens when anger has no place to go is that you turn it towards yourself. 'I'm hopeless, ugly, stupid, I should have expressed myself better, I should have found a way to escape, I should have been able to stop him' are all ways of giving yourself anger that is often intended for other people. Often people find it easier to be angry with people *outside* the family.

▷ 'The police were really insensitive.'
▷ 'I tried to tell the teacher but she was too dumb to pick up the message.'
▷ 'Passersby stood there and watched him force me in the car.'
▷ 'Eighteen months in prison is nothing – the court is hopeless.'

A lot of these angry feelings are justified. They are for people in authority, who have power and strength which could have been used to help, but wasn't.

If you manage to find them, however, it is likely that the greatest angry feelings are for people *inside* your family. Your mother who didn't manage to keep you safe and who maybe didn't believe you, or maybe abused you in other ways.

> *The time is here Mum*
> *I'm exploring your mind*
> *Yes, Mum*
> *I will find out why you were so unkind*
>
> *You made my life so cold and dark*
> *19 years without shine*
> *19 years without spark*
>
> *Sarah*

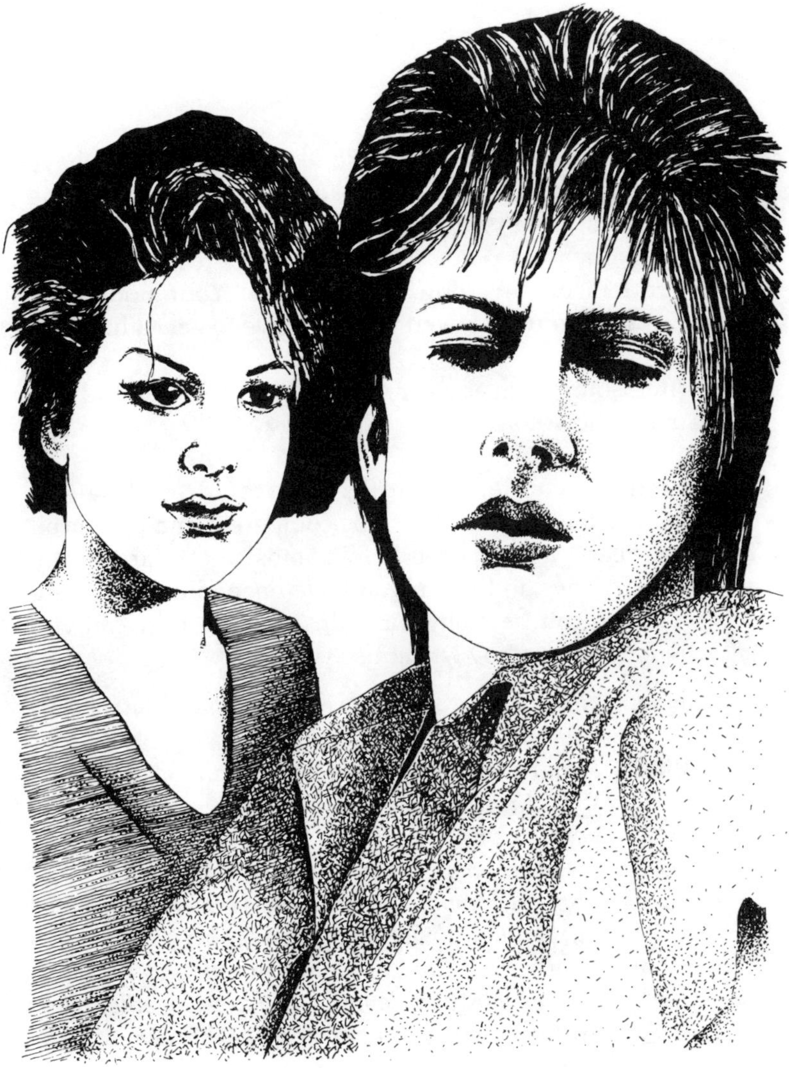

Your sister who teased you for being pathetic when she didn't realise you sacrificed yourself for her. Your brother who got off scot free and didn't understand your suffering. And the person who is really responsible – the one who abused you. It is really normal to wish he were dead, to want to hurt, castrate, or kill him, or wish he stayed in prison for ever.

Men – Yuk!

Having a bad experience with one man may well have convinced you that all men are like that. Just being in the same room as a man can be very distressing. You may be aware of your heart pounding, your palms feeling sweaty, and shudders passing down your spine. Your body may shrink away or you may even feel you have to get right out of the room.

Often something about a man you meet can remind you of the man who abused you.

At other times you may wish that you could be close to a man because men often seem to be competent and powerful. Teenage years are a time when most girls are really interested in boys and when you have been abused, getting close to a boy can be really difficult. After all, how can you tell whether or not a boy will abuse you?

> Josie: *Nice guys are more of a risk. They suck you in and then they let you down.*
>
> Alice: *I can't ever call him by name. It is the same as my stepfather's.*
>
> Rangi: *I catch glimpses of men in town who remind me of my uncle, and I run into shops and hide.*
>
> Moana: *My skin crawls all over when Michael has his top shirt buttons undone and I can see his hairy chest.*
>
> Samantha: *I can't bear to look at the butcher shoving the meat on the scales and slapping the parcel together. His big rough hands make me feel like throwing up all over his floor.*

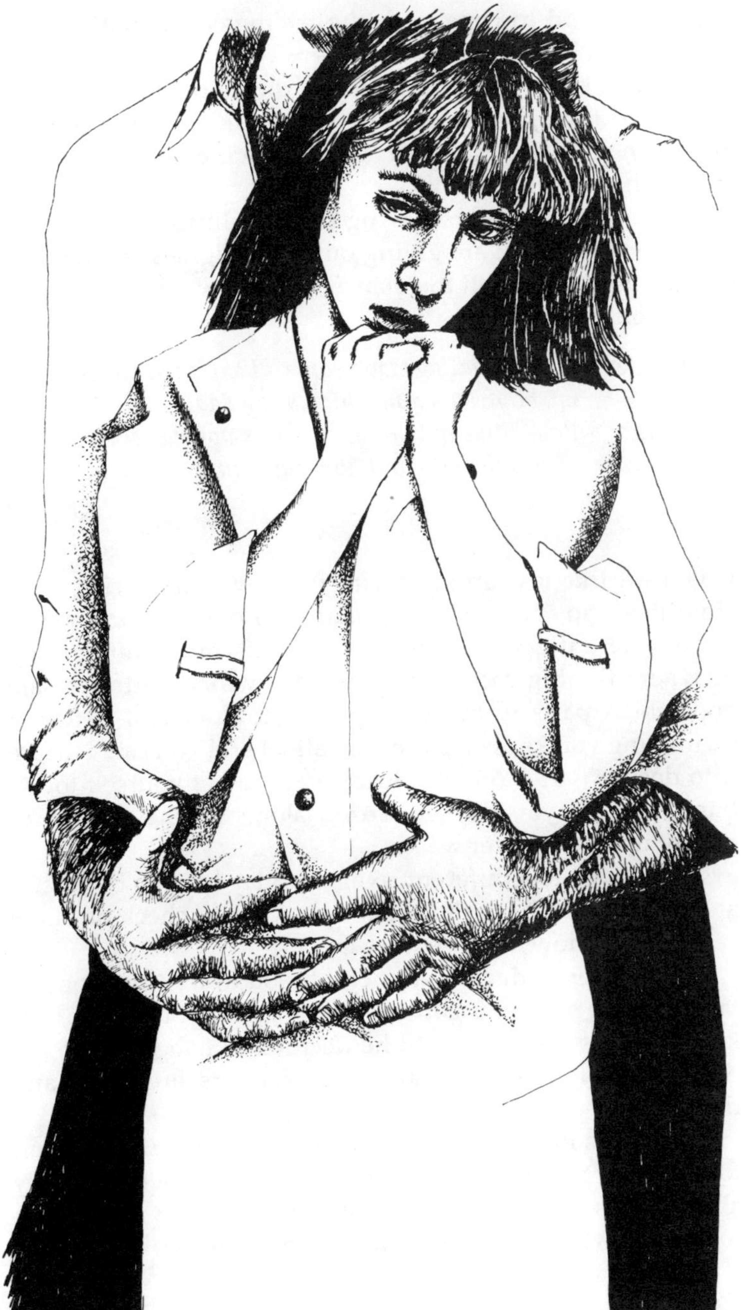

It is often hard to cope with the feelings of hatred toward men that well up inside you. One way people do this is to imagine all kinds of horrible things they would like to have happen to them, or things they would like to do to them – giving them a taste of their own medicine so they would know what you feel like.

Sometimes though, having these feelings can be scary. You may worry you are giving out some signals about what you are thinking and if the man gets to know he may want to attack you.

Natalie: *It is like dating two people – I can't tell which is my boyfriend and which is my dad.*

Sarah: *Boys come in two types – ones you can trust and ones you can't, but how can you tell which is which?*

It is a bit like learning to swim in a river. If, during your childhood, you have lots of chances to practise, you get to know where it gets too deep or too swift, murky underfoot, or where the big rocks are. You learn which parts are safe and which parts to avoid. As you get older and better at swimming you know how to stay afloat and you can venture into deeper parts. You also learn ways to get yourself to the bank, even if you do get carried along by the current or caught up in the water weed.

If you go to a different river you may have to be careful at first, but you have the skills to be able to check out how safe it is and how far to venture in.

However, if during your childhood every time you got taken to the river you got thrown in out of your depth and kept there by an adult until he decided to fish you out, the only thing you would learn is that rivers are scary and dangerous.

All girls have to use their testing out skills if they want to get close to a boy, but for girls who have been sexually abused, this is extremely difficult. It is very scary to try even to paddle, when you haven't learnt *any* water skills, because as soon as you put your feet in, you may hit a rock, or get swept away or entangled in the water weed. Staying on the bank may be lonely, but you may think it is very much safer.

Boys and young men who have been abused have to use their water skills too. But the difficulty isn't so much a problem with getting close to girls and women, as it is to do with men. Having had the experience of having sex with a man, the question might be 'Am I gay or am I straight?' and 'Will other men know and want to have sex with me as well?'

A lot of teenagers want to have friends of the opposite sex, but don't want a sexual relationship. Being constantly on guard for anything that may lead towards sex, or even any kind of closeness, however, can mean that even being friends is difficult.

Tim: *As soon as he asks me things about myself I joke, and change the subject.*
Melissa: *Dancing is fine until he wants to hold me close. Then I say I need to get a drink.*

Other teenage girls would like a sexual relationship, but find it is impossible.

Jill: *When he kisses me I want to throw up.*
Shelley: *I would like to have sex with him but as soon as we begin I get images of huge, horrible hard penises.*
Amanda: *My uncle was always violent when he had sex with me. John isn't but I keep waiting for it, on guard, ready to protect myself.*

Often boyfriends behave like men who abuse.

Suzette: *Boys want only one thing. He told me he would drop me if I didn't have sex with him.*

This attitude can often make you feel pressured into doing something you don't want, so you don't lose your boyfriend.

Even if you make it over the hurdle and get into a relationship with a boy, knowing whether or not to tell him about what has happened to you is often another huge hurdle.

> Anna: If I tell he will know I am damaged goods and he might feel it is all right to do it to me again – like being recycled.
>
> Paula: He might feel revolted, not able to handle it, and then he would leave me, but if I don't tell he won't be able to make allowances for me.

Surviving teenage years can be tricky at the best of times. For a girl, becoming a teenager involves developing relationships with males. If you have been abused, this is extremely difficult because it is males who have abused you. Getting involved with them brings back all kinds of painful memories and feelings and means you run the risk of it happening again. Not getting involved means not being like other teenagers and that is painful too.

For a boy, becoming a teenager involves developing relationships with girls. Getting involved may feel strange, and mean you still keep wondering if you are homosexual. This may mean you feel you have to work very hard to have sex often enough, with enough girls, to convince yourself you are not.

I feel I have lost everything, even myself

Fires, floods, and burglaries all cause people to suffer losses in their lives – often the loss of things that are hard to replace. What usually makes it easier to cope is that friends, neighbours and family all come running to offer support and comfort.

People who have been sexually abused often suffer losses that make fires look like a lit match, and floods like a big puddle. Unlike victims of fire and flood, friends, neighbours, and family seldom come running. Usually they don't know, and when they do they often don't believe.

The first big loss is that of childhood. If you were being sexually abused, you would have felt very different from your classmates. It is likely that carefree children's games often seemed impossible, concentration on school work difficult, and inviting classmates home an ordeal. This meant making friends was really difficult.

The second big loss is to do with your family. When you tell on him, this almost always means a disruption in the family. At worst, it means you will lose them by having to move out. At best, it means the loss of the person who has been abusing you and the loss of the way the family was before.

A third loss, which is also really scary, is the feeling that you have lost yourself. You feel like there is a hole inside you and you can't find the bits to fill it, you constantly doubt your own judgement, and feel you don't know yourself any more. Sometimes you may fear you will really fall apart and maybe you will never be able to get the pieces together again.

You may have been forced to take responsibility beyond your years:

▷ taking responsibility for Mum's peace of mind by keeping the secret
▷ taking responsibility for making Dad feel good
▷ taking responsibility for propping up parents who are struggling
▷ being more responsible for younger brothers and sisters than you ought to be.

This interferes, in a big way, with being a *kid*.

I feel responsible

I should have ....
I shouldn't have ....
If only I had ....
If I hadn't ....
I wish I had ....
It is my fault ....
I know it is not my fault, but ....

If you find you are beginning lots of sentences (either out loud or in your head) in these ways, you are probably expert at giving yourself a hard time. You may even be so good at it that you have convinced yourself that being sexually abused *was* all your fault.

> *'I shouldn't have gone to him for cuddles.'*
>
> *'I should have said I didn't want his presents.'*
>
> *'When I was little I didn't know any better, but it was my fault I let him continue when I was a teenager.'*
>
> *'If only I had made a fuss.'*
>
> *'I know it is not my fault, but then I think it must be, because he didn't abuse my sister, only me.'*
>
> *'It must be my fault. It was my grandfather who abused me. It wasn't like he was living with us. I kept going to his house. I never said I didn't want to go.'*

Thinking it is your fault probably has a lot to do with the way you have been brought up. Everyone has positive and negative parts of them. If your parents never notice the positive ones, it would have been hard for you to grow up feeling good about yourself. Even worse, if they continually commented on the negative ones, you would grow up thinking that you were bad and that whatever went wrong must be because of you.

Giving yourself messages like the ones listed are ways of punishing yourself. If you have practised punishing yourself over a long time, then, even if the abuse stops, you may not be able to.

> 'If I hadn't told, my family would still be together.'
> 'It is my fault my mother feels so awful.'

If you tell, the person who abused you may get taken to court and be punished for his actions. This is society's way of saying it is his responsibility, not yours. If you are really good at blaming yourself though, you may twist this all around, so you still end up giving yourself the responsibility.

> 'It is all my fault Dad is in prison.'
> 'Auntie Cheryl's life is really miserable because I told about Uncle John.'

You may have a list of excuses to try to get whoever abused you off the hook.

> 'He didn't realise what he was doing.'
>
> 'The trouble was he was manic depressive.'
>
> 'I didn't want him to move in with us.'
>
> 'I was so awful to him. If I had behaved like his daughter, maybe he would have behaved like my father.'

These are ways of keeping yourself responsible. The fact that he had a difficult childhood, you were rude to him, he had financial worries, or he didn't understand the importance of what he was doing, may all be important reasons, but they *do not* excuse his actions. *It was his problem, not yours.*

Right now, you may be telling yourself this isn't so, because in spite of what this book says, *you* know that you really were to blame. You know you are not like the majority of people described in this book, who have hated every minute of it. You, at the time it was happening, enjoyed it. If you ever admitted to that (which of course you couldn't bring yourself to do) then everyone would know you are just as responsible as he is.

It is a pretty convincing argument you have with yourself but there is an even better one. You may need to read this bit a number of times though, to try to let it sink in.

Feeling pleasure when your breasts, or clitoris, or vagina, or penis are being stroked and fondled is a normal way to respond. What wasn't normal was who was doing it, and the age you were, but that *doesn't* make feelings of enjoyment crazy, or make what happened your responsibility.

Another way of continuing to accept responsibility is to shield all important people from knowing.

> *'I would die before I would let my parents know.'*
>
> *'It is Dad's father who abused me. How can I tell him what his own father did?'*
>
> *'My mother thinks he is wonderful. She would be devastated.'*

It is not a teenager's job to protect parents in this way. You are responsible for lots of things in your life but your parents are not one of them. It is your parents' job to protect you.

The trouble though, with putting the responsibility where it really belongs, is that you have to acknowledge important people let you down. The really scary part of this is that it may mean they didn't care enough about you. Admitting that to yourself is enormously difficult, and it is often easier to keep accepting the responsibility yourself.

I don't know how I feel

I feel so angry, but whenever I snap and yell they tell me to control myself and not to be so unreasonable. They say being angry isn't allowed but they fight all the time.
I don't know how I feel.

Just when I am hating him so much he is really nice to me, says he is sorry, promises never to do it again, and gives me presents.
I don't know how I feel.

My father says this is what all fathers and daughters do, but I know it is wrong.
I don't know how I feel.

Life is really difficult for my mother. I try to help and I try to listen when she is upset but she keeps saying 'nobody ever helps'.
I don't know how I feel.

He told me I was his favourite but if that was true how could he hurt me?
I don't know how I feel.

I pull away when my father comes close. He says I don't love him.
I don't know how I feel.

I really want someone to love me and to hold me and make me feel I am special, but I hate having sex with him.
I don't know how I feel.

People tell me I am not responsible. If only one person abused me maybe I could believe that, but I have been abused by three. There must be something about me.
I don't know how I feel.

I try to talk about what happened and my family look blank and say 'What do you mean?'
I don't know how I feel.

I try to do things and they say I am stupid. Then I don't know what to do so I stand and do nothing and then they yell at me to get on with something.
I don't know how I feel.

Whenever I say I want to leave home they say I am too young and I can't look after myself. I am not too young to have sex but I can't look after myself.
I don't know how I feel.

Hurting yourself – 'The cut so deep'

At times you will probably feel the pain is just too much to bear any more and the only way to find peace and relief from that torment is to kill yourself.

The desperation that you feel is like being the sole survivor after your boat has sunk in the middle of the ocean and you haven't a life-jacket. You battle to stay afloat. First by kicking your legs, but they get tired. So you use your arms, for a while, but they get tired too. You try floating on your back, but that doesn't work, so you go back to kicking your legs, but they are still tired. Your arms are tired and you start to feel the cold seep in.

Even if there is a shore to get to, it feels as if you don't have enough energy to fight to stay afloat that long. Maybe it would be better to just let yourself sink and drown rather than have to suffer the pain of knowing that it must eventually happen anyway. Just let the pain be taken away, let the nightmare end.

Quite often though there is something that pushes you on to keep kicking, to keep breathing – the urge to stay alive. But staying alive means the pain continues.

Often what keeps you from killing yourself is other people. Maybe you feel that killing yourself would be hurtful for the people that are important for you, your family or friends. But staying alive for other people is a bit like only ever getting the left-overs from other people's meals.

Sometimes attempting to kill yourself is a way of trying to make someone pay for the pain they have made you suffer: 'If I kill myself he will be sorry he did it. And she will be sorry she never noticed!'

The trouble with this is that you can't guarantee how they will feel. He probably hasn't felt guilty in the past so he is unlikely to start now.

Hurting and injuring yourself is also a way of letting out some of the anger you feel toward other people. You probably don't feel it is safe to get angry with the man who did this to you, but the anger is still there. Sometimes you can give it to other people to whom it might not belong, but who are safe (who won't hurt you!), or you can turn it around and give it to yourself, because that is really safe!

Hurting yourself is also a way of letting people know about the pain and injury inside by making it visible on the outside: 'I used to take a razor-blade and make cuts on my arms so people could see I needed care.'

Sometimes it is a way of reassuring yourself that despite the feelings of deadness inside, you are alive because you can feel physical pain. It can also be a way of punishing yourself. You might feel that it was your fault that it happened in the first place – or guilty for splitting up the family.

There are many ways of deadening this pain:

Vicki: *They say sniffing glue is dangerous, but so what if I die, who cares anyway?*

Paul: *I go out riding my motorbike when I can't sleep at night. Sometimes I turn the lights off and see how far I can go.*

Maria: *I took a whole heap of pills once and went to sleep. But my sister found me and I woke up in hospital. The next day I just started feeling the same way all over again.*

Whatever the reason is for you, you have probably been or still are so desperately unhappy that injuring or killing yourself is an option you have seriously considered.

The pain that will end the pain, the cut so deep.

Ways of getting by

Sexual abuse is not a problem like having pimples, losing your job, failing your exams, or being dropped by your boy/girlfriend. It is something that affects your whole image of yourself and your feelings about every other person, and it interferes with every aspect of your life. For some people this is too overwhelming, they can't cope and they kill themselves. Most people however, find less drastic ways of coping.

1   Sweeping it under the carpet

This means not letting on to anyone, not even yourself. This isn't easy but you may manage to get it to work, possibly for years. To do so you need to be super-busy, always active, never quiet, never by yourself.

The tricky part is, though, that other things, like TV programmes or men you meet, remind you. Or the minute you stop the unwanted feelings and memories sneak up on you so you have to find something else to do or somewhere else to go or even louder music to play. The even trickier part is that it is hard to go to sleep, because if you lie down with nothing to do, the thoughts might arrive before the sleep. Even when you do manage to sleep, the thoughts won't leave you alone at night. You often have awful dreams, you may wake terrified in the night and sometimes, in the morning, it is hard to sort out what was real and what was the dream.

In spite of all this activity the feelings never really go away and often it becomes harder and harder to keep them under the carpet. You may have to make sure there are big enough things going on in your life so there is no chance those feelings can get a look in. It is a bit like dancing and jumping all over the carpet to flatten out any bumps that appear and to make sure the edges don't curl up and let out what is underneath.

On the other hand, what makes sweeping it under the carpet easy, is that lots of other people do it too. Letting themselves know the truth about what has happened to you, might be more than they can cope with, so they work just as hard as you to keep the corners from curling up. Some people do let themselves hear what has happened but make out it isn't that important. It is as if they do manage to lift the edge of the carpet but when they get too close to what is happening under there, they quickly drop it and make statements like: 'You will get over it', 'You have just got to put it behind you', or 'It will be alright once you forgive him.'

The opposite to dancing and jumping is sitting completely still in the middle of the carpet. You shut out everything that is happening around you, stare into space for hours and concentrate all your attention on the doorknob or light bulb. (You may already have had a lot of practise at this. When the abuse is taking place, lots of people 'cut their heads off from their bodies'. By getting to know the ceiling in intimate detail, you shut out what was happening to your body.) This can work really well, usually too well. The trouble is, you not only deaden the feelings about the abuse, you deaden *all* the feelings you have. You don't feel pain but you don't feel fun and laughter either. When friends make jokes and have good times you go through the motions of laughing and giggling, but can't feel laughter inside you.

Your school work goes downhill because you can't concentrate on the life cycle of the silk-worm and the doorknob at the same time.

The other dangerous part about keeping it under the

carpet is that awful things can be happening under there without your being aware of them. Mould can grow if the carpet is never aired and spread until the carpet rots, and woodworm can attack the floor boards and spread until they rot too.

Keeping all that pain inside you puts a lot of pressure on your body. Your muscles stay tense, your stomach heaves and churns, air can't easily get in or out of your lungs and after a while the strain can show in all kinds of physical illnesses. Sometimes they show on the outside like sores and rashes. Other times they happen on the inside like ulcers or an asthma attack.

The fact that you are reading this book means that you have been able to lift up the corner a bit. Some awful bits may have left you feeling really unaffected or bored. This means that you are not ready yet to lift the edge any further. When you have enough support and strength to bear the pain you will be able to pull the carpet back some more.

2   Being a shop window

Being a shop window is different from sweeping it under the carpet. It means you let *yourself* know how miserable you are, but to the rest of the world you present a colourful, well lit, bright display window. What is behind the window is a drab, dark, empty store. When people get near the entrance you have to push them away. They never get to see inside the store, and it never gets warmed up.

3   Being in sole charge

This is rather like running a restaurant on your own. You carry in the loads of food, cook the meals, wait at tables, pour the wine and wash the dishes single-handed. If you can't lift the sack of potatoes off the back of the truck, you don't ask any of the other workers to help you. Instead you painstakingly load half into another container and struggle on yourself. If you burn your hand, you don't take a break and ask someone else to help so you can hold it under the tap – instead, you wince from time to time, and carry on regardless.

If, as a child, whenever you tried to get your needs met, you got put down, laughed at, ignored, or told it was sinful to ask, you probably grew up believing the needs you had were unreasonable. Asking for things meant you left yourself open and got hurt.

Not asking for anything, even when you are really needy, is a way of protecting yourself. Not asking and expecting nothing means you can't be disappointed.

Running a restaurant single-handed though, is exhausting. Sooner or later you forget the orders, burn the food, and break the plates, and because you have told all the other staff you don't need them, there is no one to help sort out the mess.

4 Clinging on for dear life

Although this is the opposite to 'being in sole charge', clinging on for dear life is another way of coping with the same feelings of being hurt and let down.

When you have been sexually abused you are unable to defend yourself. This is because someone bigger and stronger puts some kind of pressure on you and exerts power over you. For this reason you may have grown up believing you are weak and useless, and the only way you can survive is to find someone strong and dependable to hold on to.

You may try to attach yourself with double knots or super-glue to anyone who shows any interest in you. This is likely to be scary for them and they may back off, leaving you feeling even more weak and useless.

You may, however, succeed in finding someone who is willing to let you cling, but this is eventually doomed to failure. He/she will, at some stage, feel he/she can never give enough. Your needs may be so overwhelming he/she will start to feel suffocated and want to get away to get some air. This withdrawal will be very scary for you and you will try to cling even harder. That may be just too much for the person you are clinging to and they may leave altogether. You will probably feel you cannot live without them, and once again, you will end up believing you are weak and useless.

5 Telling, but not in words

When you have felt telling in words was impossible you may have tried other ways to give people the message. Ways like running away, getting into trouble at school, stealing, telling dirty jokes and talking a lot about sex, or smearing blood on the walls. The trouble with this is that people don't always get the right message, and they may end up thinking you are a bad kid, or you have got a dirty mind, or you are just a trouble-maker.

6 Killing the pain

It is very hard to live with pain that doesn't go away and that aspirin won't fix. Maybe you have tried to kill it with drugs or alcohol or by sniffing glue. The trouble is you can never manage to kill the pain, you can only deaden it for a while. You also get left with the pain of being addicted, as well as the pain you started with.

7 Filling the hole

The wrong kind of love and the difficulties of getting close to people may have left you feeling as if you have a big empty hole inside. One way you may have tried to fill it is by eating and eating. The result of this is you get fatter and fatter and

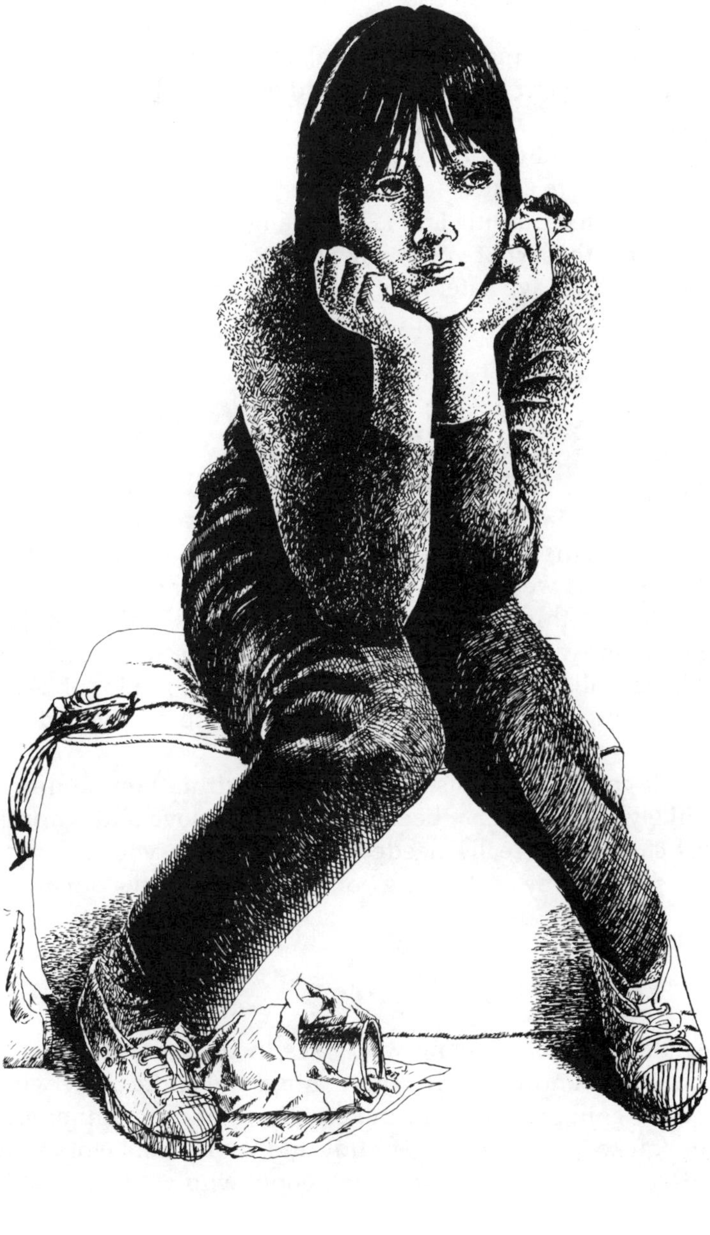

that can make you feel worse still. When that happens you feel even more empty and needy, so you comfort yourself by eating some more. Although you may not like the extra layers of fat, it may also be that they give you a kind of protection – your body is larger and more solid and that may keep men away and unwanted things out.

On the other hand, you may be so afraid of getting fat that in order to avoid that you make yourself sick after meals. (This is called bulimia and is very dangerous to your health.) It is likely that what you really want to throw up is not only the food you have eaten, but a whole heap of other stuff that is churning around in your gut.

8   Starving to death

The opposite of filling the hole is starving yourself. (This is called anorexia nervosa and you can die if you continue it for too long.) This is usually something girls do but sometimes boys do it as well. If you are a girl, by starving yourself and getting very thin you may lose your woman's shape and that may protect you from men. Your period is also a reminder of your sexuality. That sexuality so far has given a lot of pain. By starving yourself your periods may stop and you don't have this monthly reminder.

If you have been sexually abused within your family it is likely that you have been starved of the love and warmth and caring you really needed to keep inside you. Starving yourself is a way of showing your neediness on the outside.

9   Holding on tight

Maybe you are someone who likes to be super-organised. You like to know exactly where things are and exactly what you are going to do today and exactly what time dinner will be. You keep your room very tidy and your school work very orderly, and you don't tolerate people who are changeable and unpredictable. When you have been sexually abused you often feel as if you are falling apart, you will never be able to hold the bits together, and once they disintegrate you will never be able to get them back together again.

You have to hold on tight to your anger because rather than just a little coming out you may spatter it all over the walls.

You may have to hold on tight to your fears because they might never stop flowing and your whole body may be racked with sobs and shakes.

Holding on tight is a way of making sure things don't fall apart. It is often very useful but it may mean you miss out on things that 'just happen', or you get really thrown when plans get changed or things don't work out the way you had intended. You may be so busy keeping things in order, having fun may be impossible.

10 Keeping the boat steady

Being sexually abused is a bit like being in the middle of the ocean in a little dinghy, without any paddles. The wind and the weather and the tide decide what happens to you. You never know whether tonight you will be in a safe port, or at the bottom of the ocean.

Sometimes it is not possible for families to provide safe enough ports and after you have told and the abuse is over a family who can do this needs to be found for you. This safe port can be an enormous relief but often what happens is that you are still so worried about ending up at the bottom of the sea that you spend all your time trying not to rock the boat. You say very little so you won't offend people, you don't risk asking for things you need so you don't make demands on them, and you never disagree so you don't upset them.

You may be like this with friends also – always agreeing to do what they want, loaning your sweatshirt even though you wanted to wear it that night, saying it doesn't matter when they turn up late for the tenth time or don't turn up at all.

It is really important to feel safe, but if you never rock the boat even the tiniest bit, you never really get to feel any safer because you just don't know whether the boat is sturdy or not.

11 Being in the same boat

Most people have families to be attached to. Being without one that you can feel attached to is really scary and you may have used friends to compensate. You may have found others like you, without attachments. They also know what it is like to be that way, so you hold on really tightly to each other. You are all in the same boat. If you get a chance to get to a safe port that may mean abandoning your friends, and since they are the only ones who have stood by you that may feel impossible to do. The trouble is that when you keep pulling up the anchor from safe ports people think you are just a bad kid and don't want anyone to try and help you.

12 Trapped into becoming a care-giver

Being a care-giver doesn't just mean helping old people across the road or taking in stray cats. It means keeping secrets that might hurt people, being angry at yourself when you are really angry with others, telling your brother you are not hungry so he doesn't feel bad about eating the last piece of chocolate cake, spending hours listening to your friends' problems but never expecting them to listen to yours and buying presents for everyone else but never spending any money on yourself.

In families it is the adults' job to meet the children's needs. Being sexually abused by an adult, however, is a way of a child looking after an adult's needs. If things are back to front like this for you, you may think that is the way it is supposed to be. You have probably got better and better at care-giving and because you seem strong and capable you are even less likely to get your needs met. After a while you don't think having needs is reasonable. You may get annoyed with yourself for wanting even little things like love and cuddles and praise and a hand to do the dishes.

You have probably read through this book and decided that what happened to you isn't that important because worse things have happened to other people.

Giving someone else the kind of looking after you would like is often the next best thing to getting it yourself. To do this you have to find really needy people to look after. Examples of good people to choose are:

▷ someone who has had a difficult childhood and isn't coping too well
▷ someone who has got into trouble with the police and needs a hand to go straight
▷ someone who has got hooked on drugs and can't manage to get off alone.

To really specialise in caretaking you can devote your working life to it as well. The kind of jobs you might go for are nursing, teaching, missionary services, working in nurseries or old people's homes, or becoming a social worker or therapist.

Becoming a caretaker is a risky business. Caretakers often burn themselves out, and end up resenting the people they look after, and all the work they do. Usually they get taken for granted and don't get what they need anyway.

13 Sleeping around

Sleeping around seems to some people a strange thing to do – like burning your hand in the fire and continuing to put it back in. There are several good reasons though, why you may be doing this.

▷ when you have been sexually abused you often feel used and dirty. Maybe you have even been told you are 'a slut' or 'a mole' or 'a whore', and because you are a child or a teenager, you don't know any better. You probably think you really are like this. (Right now you may be thinking 'If only they really knew.') All you are doing then, is behaving the way you think you are. (It doesn't work but it is understandable.)

▷ You keep ending up having sex with someone without wanting to and without knowing why you are. You haven't, during your childhood, learnt how to avoid situations that are dangerous and uncomfortable. You can't rely on your feelings to give you warning signs, because in the past, whenever you tried to trust your feelings, you were told you were wrong.

▷ If your need to be loved isn't being met by your family you may feel empty and dead inside. In your efforts to fill yourself up you may feel you have to take all you can get – and what may be offered is sex not love. Separating the two is difficult, if not impossible, because often the messages you have been given have been very mixed up.

▷ The painful experiences of your childhood or adolescence have left you feeling helpless and powerless. One way to change that is to put yourself in a similar situation and this time try to deal with it differently. The trouble with this is that you haven't usually got the skills to manage it differently, so you keep trying and trying with one girl/boyfriend after another – changing the friend but not the skills.

14 Being a goody two shoes

If you have been sexually abused you probably feel unclean. One way to get rid of this feeling is to be a goody two shoes. This means you may act shocked when people tell dirty jokes, when your friends flirt with boys/girls, or talk about what happened in the back seat of the car. You may be impatient and irritated when classmates disrupt the class, or workmates hassle the boss or friends give their parents (and other adults) a hard time.

What you are probably trying to do is let others (and most importantly yourself) know what kind of person you are. Being a goody two shoes is an announcement that you are not dirty or a trouble-maker, and you don't (and didn't) invite sexual attention.

The trouble with this is that your classmates may think you are a prude, and if you are sensible and serious at the same time you may have to look for friends a lot older than you. Even then finding them may be difficult. Other 30-year-old teenagers are very hard to find!

15 Blending in with the wallpaper

Keeping quiet, never looking anyone in the eye, disappearing behind your desk, having a hair-style that hides your face and staying very still, are all ways of blending in with the wallpaper. In your family, this may have been a real advantage. Being invisible, so as not to be noticed, may have been the only way you could protect yourself from being yelled at, hit, or abused.

Being invisible though, means people cannot engage with you. It has been important for you to prevent *some people* engaging, but you are also preventing people engaging with you in positive ways. Wallpaper is not good company.

16 Standing out like a sore thumb

Shaving your head, dying your hair purple, wearing way-out clothes, and doing crazy things in public are all ways of making yourself stand out. This is the opposite of blending in with the wallpaper, but can have the same effect. By being outrageous and different, you keep yourself separate from other people. You may have needed to do this in order to survive, but continuing to do so could be very lonely. Other 'sore thumbs' might be better company than wallpaper, but they tend to be very difficult to live with.

17 Keeping the lid on the pressure cooker

Coping with angry feelings is very difficult because usually you have no place to put them. It often isn't safe or possible to give them to the people they are really meant for. Often someone else gets them. Then you may feel guilty so you try harder to keep them inside. After a while when people annoy you you are never sure whether the anger you are feeling is *really* for them or the person who abused you. If you can't sort this out you may end up keeping all anger inside or giving it to yourself. Harming yourself in some way like tattooing yourself, piercing your own ears, picking at your skin till it bleeds, bashing your fist or your head against the wall are all ways of causing pain or damage to yourself, when what you would really like to be doing is causing pain and damage to the person who abused you.

18 Creating a war zone

This can happen if the pressure inside the cooker gets too great and you just have to explode. Sometimes there may just be border skirmishes, after which one or other person backs down. However, when feelings run too high, full-scale war can develop.

War could be avoided if both people were able to listen to each other's point of view and negotiate. If one person is not willing to do this then the other can't either.

Being sexually abused and having all your rights as a child and teenager sabotaged is likely to make you furious. If you are not listened to on top of this, sometimes it seems that all that is left is full-scale war. Throwing plates and overturning tables may not be what you want either, but you already know talking and negotiating doesn't work in your family.

Running away, or brushing with the law, is also a way of declaring war on parents who did nothing to keep you safe.

The trouble with creating a war zone is that you may be written off as a bad kid and be seen as a threat in the family (or even in the neighbourhood) and no one may have any idea of what your battle is about.

Other people may tell you that your behaviour is crazy (even though people who have not been sexually abused often use some of these ways too). You too may wonder about whether you are 'alright in the head'.

Some of these ways of getting by may seem crazy, but sometimes acting crazy in a crazy situation is the only sane thing to do.

What you are doing is trying to find a way that works to get rid of the pain. You didn't know before you tried that none of these ways would work, so you had to try them for yourself.

But there are better ways.

What you can do now

A road map you can use

Up until now, at least some of what you have read in this book, may have related to you or someone you are close to. Not very much of it has been pleasant, and maybe you are wondering whether, as the things that have happened are so awful and difficult, it would ever be possible to feel good about yourself again. The answer is yes.

It is possible that you can start to feel differently about yourself and begin to feel whole again. It is not an easy 'yes' though. It is hard work to try and recover some of those good feelings about yourself. In a way, it is like climbing a mountain. There is strange new territory to travel through, difficulties to overcome, and a lot of energy is needed. As you climb higher there will be times when you will need to stop and rest, times when you may slip and be afraid you will fall from the mountain, times when you may feel lost, and times you wish you had never set off.

But if you keep going and reach the peak, the journey will be worthwhile. It is possible for things to be different.

It can be a hard and difficult journey if you are on your own and aren't sure which direction to go in, or where to start. So this chapter is a bit like a map. A map to show you good places to begin and where to get what you will need for the journey. Most importantly it is about how not to be alone along the way. There are people who can help. There are also a lot of girls, boys, women, and men out there, making the same journey.

First here is a brief look at the map and then we will look a bit closer at the separate parts.

1. Stop lying to yourself and others that it is not a problem.
2. Stop managing so 'well' and controlling yourself.
3. Become 'selfish'.
4. Recognise your own 'self worth'.
5. Challenge your fears.
6. Get some help.

This probably sounds like a list of impossible tasks. But if you seriously want to survive the incest experience and begin to live as a whole person without continuously being eaten up by shame and anger and unhappiness, then you will have to go through with these points. So let us take a closer look at them.

1 Stop lying to yourself

'It isn't that important.'
'It could be worse.'
'He won't do it again.'

Sweeping it under the carpet isn't only done by others, but something you probably do to yourself. The first step in stopping lying to yourself is to admit that it is important, it is awful, and that even if you think he won't do it again, the fact that he has already done it is enough.

Telling may be the hardest thing you ever have to do, but you can't begin to heal until you do. Here are some ideas of how to go about it.

Tips for telling:

a Your mother is going to find the news difficult. Often it is a good idea to tell some *outside* your family first so you have somebody to support you. Choosing a friend is a good idea but it is also important to find an adult who can take charge if you need him/her to.

b   Choose who you tell carefully. Good people to tell are teachers, school counsellors, social workers, police, doctors, and ministers. Even though you have chosen carefully, however, you can never be 100% sure that the person will be of use to you. A lot of adults want to pretend sexual abuse doesn't happen much, or isn't that important. A lot are very well meaning but simply don't *know* what to do. If the first time doesn't work, it is not your fault and it is important to try again, hard though that might be.

c   This is what should happen when you tell:
You should feel listened to and understood and believed.
The person should tell you you are doing the right thing by telling.
The person should inform the police for you or encourage you to do it.
S/he should, if you want them to, stay with you, or arrange for someone else to stay with you while the police interview you and your family.
If it is not safe to go home s/he should arrange somewhere for you to stay until things are sorted out.
S/he should let you know s/he will be in touch again soon, or if that is not possible find another person who *is* available to support you.

d   Other people finding out does not mean *you* are bringing shame on your family. It means they are getting to know about the shameful things that *were already going on*.

e   If it is possible for you to insist that he stop, do so, but don't insist that he stop *because* you will tell. He will become upset and rejected and point out all the times he has stood up for you and ask you how you can possibly think of doing this to him. Then you will feel bad and you won't be able to go through with it.

He might tell you it will be the death of your mother and you will feel convinced he is right and not go through with it.

He might tell you people will know you agreed to do it with him and he knows you have been enjoying it too, and you will feel too ashamed to go through with it.

Or he might tell you you are being unreasonable and pathetic and you will start to wonder if he is right and not go through with it.

f   There will be times when you wish you hadn't told. Times when it seems the pain and the difficulties have only been increased with no end to them, and you will wish you could take it all back. Although it is normal to feel this way, it will be worthwhile in the end.

Once you have told, it is important to keep being honest with yourself. It is often tempting to try to cover your feelings up again.

'I should be over it by now.'
'Worse has happened to others.'
'I should just forget the past and get on with the future.'

The trouble with trying to bury the pain and hurt is that unless it is dead it is going to keep coming up again. ('The return of the living dead!') It is not going to work, you will have to keep on using up your energy day after day to keep your feelings buried.

Bringing them out, feelings you may have hidden even from yourself for a long time, is going to be painful. But you need to bring them out in the open so you can see them and do something with them – to lay them to rest. Otherwise they will haunt you like ghosts from the past.

It is possible to deal with your feelings – even the really strong ones like hate and feelings of wanting to kill him or yourself. They are scary, but you can survive them, and this is best done with a therapist.

2 Stop managing so 'well' and controlling yourself

This is a bit like telling yourself 'I should be over it' and 'I should be getting on with life, not thinking about the past'.

You have probably had to hold yourself together inside so you didn't fall apart for a very long time. You have kept 'the secret', you have pretended that everything is 'just fine' and 'really I'm okay', when it really hasn't been fine and okay. But you have managed to cover that up and pretend so that nobody found out what was really going on. Maybe you did this so that people you loved wouldn't get hurt or because it seemed *you* would be destroyed by revealing what was happening *to* you and *inside* you.

Whatever the reasons, you 'managed well' and kept the lid on the boiling pot. To get yourself out of the boiling pot means you will have to take the lid off. You are going to have to stop making sure no one finds out that you have and/or are being sexually abused. This is going to upset others as well as yourself. It is not your responsibility, however, to protect your parents. They are adults, and even though it may seem like they can't look after themselves, it is not your job to do it. You need to look after yourself too and putting up with the pain and the 'shame' of the abuse isn't doing that. It is time to stop putting up with it. It is time to stop managing so well. You owe it to yourself to take the lid off.

3 Become 'selfish'

'Become selfish? Who me? I can't do that!'

Being selfish isn't always bad. It often just means putting yourself first.

'I would like to watch a programme on the other channel.'
'I can't babysit on Wednesday, I have got my judo class.'

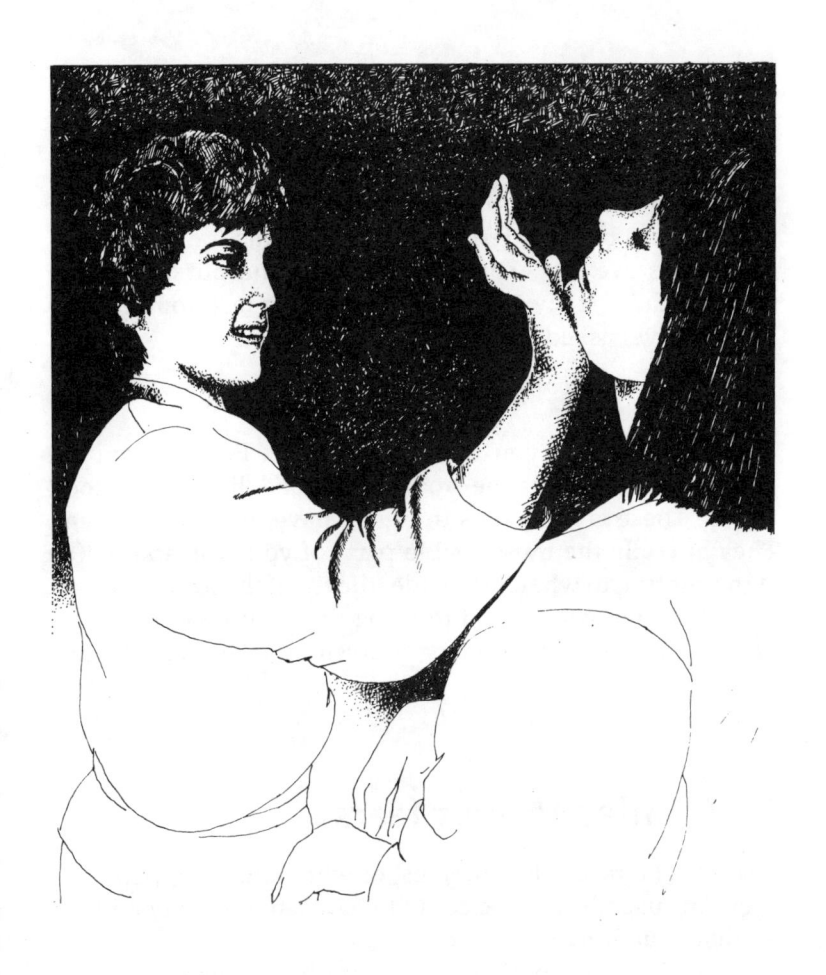

Taking time for yourself may not be easy for you. Talking to someone about yourself may feel like being selfish and you may tell yourself you don't deserve it. Time for yourself though, is something everyone has the right to have. It is an important, healthy thing you need to give yourself. Allowing yourself to be cared for is like being a garden and being tendered and watered so that you grow and flower, instead of always being the gardener and doing all the hard work.

4 Recognise your own 'self worth'

'How do I do that?'

It is like the deserving part of 'becoming selfish' – the part of you that has been suffering pain and shame for so long but *doesn't* deserve that! You have survived and put up with so much already, really what you deserve is a rest from it. After all, *you* never asked for any of this to happen.

'But I'm not worth anything!'

There are parts of you that are valuable. Perhaps you are good at sport or maybe you are a good listener, a good friend. These are precious things to have, hang on to them. They are only the most visible parts of your valuable self, a sign pointing to what lies inside, the tip of the iceberg.

It is time you started to recognise your own value as a person. So take some time for yourself because *you are worth it!*

5 Challenge your fears

Fears are fantasies, like dreams, of what might happen. And they are usually connected with what has happened in a similar situation in the past.

For instance, perhaps you were bitten by a dog when you were young. Well, probably now you are scared of big dogs because you fear that they will bite you. That is quite wise, because not going anywhere near dogs will ensure you don't get bitten again. You will have to work hard all your life though to make sure you are never near dogs. Phew! Sounds like a lot of effort.

Here is another example. You were sexually abused by a man, now you are going to be really wary of any man for fear that he too will abuse you. That is also quite wise, after all, how can you trust any of them when the one who was supposed to protect and care for you most took advantage of you?

The trouble is, being afraid of men and having to ensure that you are safe from them (and this might mean ensuring that you are never alone with a man) is going to take heaps of energy, for ever.

These are just some examples of fears, perhaps you have different ones. But you know what they are, after all, they are there day after day, night after night.

Well, for things to change, you have to spend less time and energy worrying about protecting yourself from what *might* happen. You are going to have to meet your fears. This is going to be scary, and difficult, and you may only be able to do little bits at a time. It might be important for you not to feel alone when you do it. Having someone there you know, and can trust, will probably be necessary for you to feel safe enough to 'challenge' your fears and find out what they are really like. And also to find out what you are like when you meet them.

You may be surprised!

6 Get some help

Going it alone is going to be *really* difficult and asking for help doesn't mean you have failed. You will be left with a whole lot of feelings that may be impossible to sort out alone. You are going to need support, someone to share the load with, someone who knows 'where to go next' when you feel lost or tired. You'll need someone to journey up your mountain with you. Get yourself a therapist or counsellor. Usually a doctor or social worker will be able to put you in touch with one.

Accepting help from someone else is going to be risky, though. It means looking at painful feelings and experiences.

Probably the most difficult part will be trusting someone else with those parts of yourself that you don't feel good about, showing someone the 'rotten' bits. It is scary because it seems the risk is always there that they may not like you. The fear, however, is usually greater than the reality.

Even when you do get to trust your therapist the worst isn't over. Liking someone and allowing them to be important to you can be scary, because you fear that, if you let them become too important, you will never be able to do without them.

You will need to check out your counsellor carefully and slowly, bringing out 'little bits' of yourself, at a rate that is not going to overwhelm you. It's a bit like getting in at the shallow end of the swimming pool and wading into the deep water – rather than saying too much too soon which is like leaping into the deep water before you know if you can swim.

Go slowly. It is going to take quite a while but it can work.

Sophie: *I used to be all screwed up like a piece of paper in the rubbish bin. I've gradually unfolded and although I'll always have the creases in me, now I'm too important to ever end up in the bin again.*

Paul: *At times I cried and cried and it seemed too painful. But letting out the tears made a space inside of me and that meant good things could come in.*

Angela: *Now I'm as tall as everyone else.*

This plan is by no means a complete, do-it-yourself, foolproof, super-duper guarantee to solve all problems! It still requires you to come up with some creative new ways to deal with your own situation. You have done that before, so you can do it again, only this time it will be a little different.

What this chapter is about is that 'different' way of handling the situation. It is going to be painful and require energy. But it will lead to a whole new ending to a story which hasn't been happy so far. The choices for this ending are really important because they are yours.

Glossary of terms

Anus: (slang words – arsehole, bum) The opening of the rectum or large intestine to the outside. Your bowel motions pass out through this hole. A man putting his penis in a man or woman's anus is also a way of having sex (called sodomy or buggery).

Breasts: (slang words – tits, boobs, knockers) The milk secreting organs on a woman's chest. During puberty girls' breasts and nipples get bigger and the dark area round the nipple areola (pronounced aree-o-la) also gets larger and darker.

Clitoris: Pronounced clit-or-iss. The most sensitive part of a girl's sex organs. It is about the size of a pea and pokes out of a hood of skin at the top of the vulva where the inner lips meet.

Crotch: Pronounced crutch. The area between the top of your legs including your genitals (sex organs).

Erection: When a boy or man gets sexually excited the muscles at the base of the shaft tighten and blood flows into the veins and not out. This makes his penis swell up and become erect.

Genitals: Male or female sex organs. For a woman this includes the vagina and clitoris; for a man, the penis and scrotum.

Intercourse: (slang words – fucking, screwing, laying) The technical term is coitus, pronounced coy-tuss . This is when a male puts his erect penis inside a female's vagina. In the case of sexual abuse this is something a man does *to* a girl or woman. In a loving relationship it is something men and women do *with* each other for enjoyment.

Incest: See page 99 (where we already have a definition).

Masturbate: Pronounced mass-ter-bate (slang words – wanking, playing with yourself, jerking off – for boys). Rubbing your clitoris or penis in order to get sexually excited and often to give yourself an orgasm. Masturbation can give you a good feeling. It can also make it easier for you to enjoy sex with someone else because once you know how your body responds it will be easier for you to show your sexual partner what is right for you.

Orgasm (or climax): (slang word – coming) You can have an orgasm either by masturbating or having sex with someone else. It is what happens when our feelings of sexual excitement build up to a high level. At the peak, the sex organs contract in a series of spasms. This is a feeling of release and enjoyment which flows through your whole body. When males reach a climax semen comes spurting out of the hole at the tip of their penis. The penis goes limp almost immediately and their bodies get back to being relaxed.
Females can have several orgasms in a row with only a few seconds in between.
When a couple are having sex together either one or both may have an orgasm. When a man uses a woman or a girl for his own needs as in sexual abuse, he is the only one who has an orgasm.

Pads or sanitary pads: These are usually made of absorbent cotton and have an adhesive strip so they stick to a girl's pants and absorb the blood when she is having a period.

Penis: (slang names – cock, dick, prick) A male sexual organ also used for urinating. The penis is made up of two parts – the head, called the glans, and the long part, the shaft.

Period: (slang words – monthly, misery). The part of the menstrual cycle in which girls, after reaching the stage of puberty, bleed for two to eight days. This necessitates the wearing of tampons or pads to absorb the blood.

Pubic hair: The hair that grows around male and female sex organs.

Scrotum: (slang words – balls, bollocks, nuts) Pouch which hangs down behind the penis, containing the testicles, a pair of glands which produce sperm and male sex hormones.

Sexuality: Pronounced sex-u-al-it-ee. The feeling or sensation of sexual attraction you may have towards another person – the feeling of being sexually aroused without necessarily engaging in sexual activity. A sense of your own ability to become involved sexually with yourself or another person.

Tampons: Small finger-like wads of cotton wool. They are pushed into the vagina where they expand to absorb the flow of blood.

Vagina: A female's sexual passage from the uterus to the outside. It is normally about 9 cm long but can stretch both lengthwise and widthwise.

Useful Addresses – Seeking Help

Many of the national organisations listed below also have regional offices, check the telephone directory for local information.

CHILDLINE
Faraday Building
Queen Victoria Street
London EC4 4BU
Tel: 0800–1111

GINGERBREAD – LONE PARENT AND CHILD SUPPORT AGENCY
35 Wellington Street
London WC2E 7BN
Tel: 071–240 0953/0954

INCEST CRISIS LINE
66 Marriott Close
Bedfont
Feltham
Middlesex
Tel: 081–890 4732

LONDON RAPE CRISIS CENTRE
P.O. Box 69
London WC1X 9NJ
Tel: 071–278 3956 or 071–837 1600

NATIONAL ASSOCIATION OF YOUNG PEOPLE'S COUNSELLING AND ADVISORY SERVICE (NAYPCAS)
17–23 Albion Street
Leicester LE1 6GD
Tel: 0533–558763

NATIONAL CHILDREN'S BUREAU
8 Wakely Street
London EC1V 7QE
Tel: 071–278 9441

NATIONAL COUNCIL FOR ONE PARENT FAMILIES
255 Kentish Town Road
London NW5 2LX
Tel: 071–267 1361

NATIONAL SOCIETY FOR THE PREVENTION OF CRUELTY TO CHILDREN (NSPCC)
67 Saffron Hill
London EC1N 8RS
Tel: 071–242 1626

RELATE (MARRIAGE GUIDANCE)
Herbert Gray College
Little Church Street
Rugby CV21 3AP
Tel: 0788–73241

ROYAL SCOTTISH SOCIETY FOR THE PREVENTION OF CRUELTY TO CHILDREN (RSSPCC)
4 Polworth Terrace
Edinburgh EH1 3QR
Tel: 031–337 8539

SCOTTISH CHILD AND FAMILY ALLIANCE (SCAFA)
56 Albany Street
Edinburgh EH1 3QR
Tel: 031–557 2780

All the following numbers can be found in your local telephone directory

EDUCATION WELFARE OFFICER
Listed under the Education section of County Council

HEALTH VISITOR
Listed under Health Authority or name of GP

POLICE
Listed under 'Police' – do not use the 999 number unless it is an emergency

SOCIAL SERVICES
Listed under name of City or County Council – ask for the Duty Social Worker

The authors: David Carlyle and Joy Hayward
(Photograph: Liz Price)